The roots of populism

Manchester University Press

The roots of populism

Neoliberalism and working-class lives

Brian Elliott

MANCHESTER UNIVERSITY PRESS

Published by Manchester University Press
Altrincham Street, Manchester M1 7JA

www.manchesteruniversitypress.co.uk

British Library Cataloguing-in-Publication Data
A catalogue record for this book is available from the British Library

ISBN 978 1 5261 3697 8 hardback

First published 2021

Typeset by
Servis Filmsetting Ltd, Stockport, Cheshire

Contents

Introduction

Since the Brexit referendum result in the UK and the election of Donald Trump in the US in 2016, 'populism' has become one of the keywords of contemporary political discourse. Both events have precipitated a predictable torrent of writing, both in the popular media and in academia. The underlying consensus across these accounts is that populism represents, at base, a cardinal threat to the values and possibly even the continued existence of democratic culture. This threat is often articulated in terms of an extreme polarizing between 'Us' and 'Them' within political logic and representation. As Cas Mudde (2018) notes: 'Most scholars use populism as a set of ideas focused on an opposition between the people (good) and the elite (bad).' To the extent that the Brexit (British exit from the EU) referendum result is recognized as a key symptom of British populism, this is similarly viewed as a largely negative protest vote. As William Davies, who has written extensively on populism for the *Guardian* and in monographs, remarks, 'it seems clear that – beyond the rhetoric of "Great Britain" and "democracy" – Brexit was never really articulated as a viable policy, and only ever as a destructive urge, which some no doubt now feel guilty for giving way to' (Davies, 2016: 22).

Finally, academic studies of populism predominantly accentuate linkages with nativism, xenophobia and right-wing extremism (see Miller-Idriss and Pilkington, 2019; Norris and Inglehart, 2019; Traverso, 2019). In the US, following Donald Trump's presidential victory, this is often accounted for in terms of an ongoing backlash against the rise of 'liberal values'. As Pippa Norris (2016) noted in the run-up to Donald Trump's presidential election campaign: 'Trump's support appears to be fueled by a backlash among traditionalists (often men and the less educated) faced with rising American support for issues such as gay marriage, sexual equality, and tolerance of social diversity' (Norris, 2016). While I do not deny there is a degree of truth to these academically hegemonic treatments of populism, I align my analysis with another, quite distinct interpretation.

In this book, I argue that populism should be chiefly viewed as a reassertion of the original demand that gave rise to modern democracy. That demand is that the working class – a notion I will elaborate on in what follows – have visible, credible and generalized control over the material conditions of social existence, including control over the conditions of work. Accordingly, the thesis of this book is that populism should not be seen, at base, as a threat to but rather as a reassertion of modern democratic culture. Thus, it is not a question of populism *or* democracy, but rather populism within and for the sake of democracy.

In order to make this argument plausible, it will be necessary to characterize in detail those aspects of populism that are consistent with a reassertion of the cardinal democratic demand. Thus, while the analysis advanced in this book does not contest the claim that the current populist wave is in part motivated by nativist and nationalistic sentiments, it deliberately focuses on what might crudely be called the non-oppressive, properly democratic intent I contend underlies populism. If, on the contrary, populism is seen exclusively as an anti-liberal and anti-democratic political trend, then the idea that it represents a valid critique of the current state of liberal democracy is precluded in advance. My hope is that the underlying argument of this book is sufficiently novel to be engaging, but not so eccentric as to seem insupportable.

How then *can* populism be seen as a reassertion of the original democratic impulse? The key insight here is to view the rise of populism in the twenty-first century as an adverse reaction not to social liberalization but rather to economic and cultural *neo*liberalization. Accordingly, it is a matter of demonstrating how the shift to neoliberal governance, in the UK and other liberal democracies in the early 1980s, involved a political project inherently opposed to democracy understood as popular control over material conditions. Since that time, the norm of a self-determining collective democratic citizenry has been displaced by what Foucault, in a series of lectures delivered in 1979, notably characterized as a political-economic regulative ideal of the individual as 'entrepreneur of himself' (2008: 226). This involves an ideological as well as an institutional shift. Rather than allowing the populace to become self-organizing and self-determining social agents, neoliberal governance permits collective self-determination only within the framework of consumption-based corporate monopoly capitalism. Under the neoliberal aegis, workers are asked time and again to sacrifice the desire to control their own conditions of existence to the needs of an anonymous national and global economy. Eclipsing and dissolving the political into a particular paradigm of the economic is a salient hallmark of neoliberalism.

Progressively alienated from a two-hundred-year-old legacy of agitation and self-organization, under neoliberalism the working class in the UK and other liberal democracies has experienced the collapse of traditionally left-leaning political parties into mere creatures of hegemonic corporate interests. This process reached a transparently grotesque point when the 2008 Great Recession hit. At this point, the lurid contrast between homeowners being evicted due to defaulting on their mortgage loans and bank CEOs (chief executive officers) netting millions of dollars in bonuses become socially explosive. The Occupy movement was the most visible expression of popular outrage. But this was, ultimately, short-lived and lacked the coherent political demands needed to generate a movement with staying power and the clout to change the political system fundamentally. This book is far from unique in highlighting the pivotal interconnections between the Great Recession, neoliberalism and the rise of liberal democratic populism (see Judis, 2016). What is more distinctive about the analysis offered here, however, is its recognition that populism carries within it an appeal to the original and radical demand of democracy in the form of popular control over social existence.

From the perspective of British social history, the time span of neoliberalism is roughly the time of my own life. I was born in 1969 into a working-class family in northern England. My parents knew first-hand the deprivations of working-class poverty growing up in Liverpool in the 1930s and 1940s, years of economic recession followed by the straightened circumstances of the wartime and immediate post-war economy. They married in the 1950s and left their home city – extensively bombed and subsequently significantly depopulated – on the promise of better-paid work and a council home on the other side of the Mersey. Given this background, the personal motivation in writing this book is twofold. First, it represents an acknowledgement of the kinds of working-class culture in which I grew up. This culture is sharp-witted and caustic, involving close social ties and a general cynicism about the world beyond itself. Growing up, I felt this working-class milieu to be narrow-minded, incurious and stultifying. I think I can now see its merits in a way I could not forty or even twenty years ago.

Second, and closely related to the first point, I feel called upon to validate certain aspects of the working-class culture as embodied by my parents and grandparents. My grandparents on my father's side spent the last twenty years of their lives living in a council-owned tower block in Childwall, Liverpool. In my recollections of childhood, they seemed perfectly content to be living in their modest two-bedroom council flat. They neither owned their home nor did they wish to. They knew most people in the block and the surrounding area. They went about their daily round with a kind of modest contentment: visiting and being visited by friends and family, with the occasional trip to the local shops, the bowling club or the bookmakers. Summer holidays consisted of a week or so at a Butlin's holiday camp on the North Wales coast. For my younger self, my grandparents' home represented a magically serene world, where nothing seemed to happen but everything was filled with a quiet joy. The paradox of this, when I now look back, is that my grandparents had virtually nothing in material goods and wealth and yet never seemed to miss or desire them. For my part, the seemingly endless offering of biscuits and cakes, punctuated by plentiful cups of tea, was already unimagined riches to my seven-year-old self.

This personal experience informs a crucial further claim advanced in this book: the working class is injured just as much, if not more so, by lack of political recognition as by economic deprivation. This is a central plank of the neoliberal transformation: that working-class practices of solidarity are dissolved within the social ideology of individualized self-betterment. To some extent, this change can be captured in terms of the working class embracing an aspiration for more typically middle-class lifestyles and possessions. But it is insufficient to portray the social and cultural impact of neoliberalization as a mere transition from working-class to middle-class values. As the central chapters of this book will argue, it is the working-class's sense of being overlooked, ignored and thereby denigrated which has played a crucial role in giving rise to the widespread populist sentiment we now see on display in the UK and elsewhere. This is not to say that racism and xenophobia are not hallmarks of contemporary British working-class culture. But such mental attitudes are largely effects and not causes, compensatory mechanisms that respond to the reality of lacking social and political recognition. In a word, populism should be understood as arising from a demand, largely unstated and unrecognized, for the working class to regain social-political visibility and dignity.

The following analysis focuses largely on contemporary UK populism. I am aware that, given the international political conjuncture, this limits its potential validity. The immediate reason for this limitation is personal: I was born, raised and educated in the UK. For the last decade I have lived and worked in the United States (in Portland, Oregon), and this allows me more of an experiential foothold in US domestic politics. But, in this book, the focus remains largely on populism within British politics. Within this context, neoliberalization can be seen to reach a certain stage of maturity with the ascent of a reformulated Labour Party. The British Labour Party under Tony Blair rebranded itself as 'New Labour', thereby alienating its traditional working-class electorate by emphasizing a break with the workers' movements of the nineteenth and twentieth centuries, with socialism and with the labour unions.

Party pluralism in the context of a liberal democracy is not a matter of simply having different products on the shelf to choose from. Rather, the different parties are necessary to articulate real differences of material interest within the political community. When the British Labour Party replaced the Liberal Party, which had championed political democratization throughout most of the nineteenth century, it represented the culmination of over a hundred years of working-class organization and agitation. Rebranding the party as New Labour sent out a clear message that the Thatcherite neoliberal transition was now ideologically unopposed by the two major political parties. As Panitch and Leys (2001: 290) tellingly noted after the first term of Blair's New Labour, 'the lack of party alternatives is now felt as strongly by the British left as it has always been by the American left'. In hindsight, we can now see that New Labour's historic run of three electoral victories between 1997 and 2005 was bought at the price of leaving the British working class effectively homeless within the UK's party-political system. This was the crucial development that opened a space for contemporary British populism, expressed initially in significant electoral results for the UK Independence Party (UKIP) led by Nigel Farage and later by the surge of support for Brexit.

The decade following the defeat of Gordon Brown as Labour's leader in the general election campaign of 2010 witnessed thoroughgoing economic austerity, presided over initially by a Conservative–Liberal Democrat coalition government. The Occupy Wall Street (OWS) movement that arose in the US in the midst of the Great Recession in September 2011 was the most salient social-political reaction to fiscal austerity. Shortly before, there had been a precursor to this in the UK where, in August 2011, London experienced repeated waves of public rioting and looting. Thomas Piketty's (2013) book *Capital in the Twenty-First Century* became an unlikely best-seller two years later. Both the 'We are the 99%' slogan of OWS and Piketty's meticulous analysis of inexorable economic inequality highlighted the distributive justice dimension to the neoliberal transformation. While the present analysis does not contest the important role played by exacerbated economic inequality over the preceding decade, it focuses rather on the qualitative dimension of how the working class under neoliberal hegemony has been rendered socially invisible and politically inaudible. In other words, the underlying cause of contemporary populism in the UK is presented in terms of the 'hidden injuries' (Sennett and Cobb, 1972) inflicted upon the working class under conditions of advanced neoliberal governance.

Accordingly, in this book contemporary populism is presented as an inchoate and largely blind reassertion of the principle of popular sovereignty within the democratic polity. In this light, the narrow victory of those who voted for the UK to leave the European Union should be seen as a symptom rather than the cause of a crisis in British democracy. The virtual paralysis of the UK government between 2016 and 2019 demonstrated, in turn, how difficult the British political class finds it to put into effect 'the will of the people'. The two general elections that occurred in those years found all major parties vying to win over various subsets of the populace that had voted roughly 50/50 for and against continued membership of the EU. The Conservatives under Theresa May were divided against themselves (as they have been on the question of Europe since the 1980s). Labour, for its part, attempted an ultimately disastrous balancing act that saw its seats at Westminster plummet alarmingly in the 2019 general election under the leadership of Jeremy Corbyn.

Amidst the parliamentary pyrotechnics of those years, within the political establishment there seemed little genuine reflection on how the combined efforts of the political and economic establishment had come to be defeated in a popular vote in 2016. Caught up in the customary short-termism of electoral politics, the political class failed to recognize crucial elements of meaning connected to the Brexit vote. This lack of radical political reflection is, I believe, symptomatic of the depoliticization of British liberal democracy itself. Under the auspices of neoliberal reason, this depoliticization takes the form of an unquestioning economism with regard to all matters of social value. Brexit was considered by the political establishment a bad decision because it would be bad for business. When pro-EU opponents of Brexit within the political establishment found it unaccountable that the British working class could remain unconvinced by this line of argument, they failed to see that the neoliberal ideological identification between market buoyancy and collective self-interest had been terminally undermined in the aftermath of the 2008 financial crisis. Accordingly, Brexit voters found it relatively easy to subordinate economic growth to what promised to offer an enhanced sense of dignity and recognition. This preference for recognition over economics is why 'Take back control' was such an effective rhetorical rallying call on both sides of the Atlantic in 2016.

While the 2008 financial crisis offers a proximate cause of the recent wave of populism, the underlying causes derive from the neoliberal transformation which began in the 1970s and became conspicuously present by the early 1980s. In broad terms, the argument advanced in this book aligns with Paul Mason's (2015) claim that the hegemony of neoliberal governance has interrupted a necessary transition out of the phase of capitalism that began in the immediate post-Second World War period. Liberal democratic politics feels as though it has been in a kind of holding pattern since the hegemony of the Washington Consensus emerged in the 1990s, following the collapse of the Soviet Union and its variety of command and control economics. However, whereas Mason (2015) believes a politically progressive framework of advanced automation holds the key to releasing Western democracies from the shackles of neoliberalism, the argument advanced in this book calls for a reformulation of the concrete contexts of working-class solidarity and popular sovereignty, including a holistic and credible reconstituting of mass union organization and worker-owned and -controlled business. Clearly, this cannot come in the form of an implausible 'back to the future' scenario. Working-class politics of the twenty-first century cannot be a mere rehash of nineteenth- and twentieth-century socialism and social democracy.

In terms of methodological approach, this is a work of political theory: it does not harbour any pretensions to original social science research, nor it is primarily based on collated social science data. My immediate academic background is in philosophy, more specifically in twentieth-century European philosophy. The strength of my approach to the phenomenon of populism in this book is, arguably, also its weakness; namely, a more speculative methodology largely based on prolonged reflection. The political theory applied here to frame the contemporary phenomenon of populism is derived from an extended engagement with the logic of neoliberal governance. This began with an attempt at a critique of managerial local democratic governance in my book *Constructing Community* (Elliott, 2010) and was more directly developed in a critical analysis of the politics of climate change in the age of 'sustainable development' in *Natural Catastrophe* (Elliott, 2016). The itinerary of my thinking during this period has been guided chiefly by the work of the contemporary Marxist geographer David Harvey and the cultural and social theorist Raymond Williams. The spirit of their thinking animates the analysis of populism offered throughout this book.

Part of the impetus to write this work stems from a frustration at what struck me as the preponderant, simplified reactions to Brexit in particular and, secondarily, to the election of Donald Trump. As Eatwell and Goodwin note in their thorough and incisive analysis of contemporary populism: 'People tend to reduce highly complex movements to "one type" of voter or "one cause" because they want simple and straightforward explanations' (2018: 17). As the UK general elections of 2017 and 2019 went on to show, the causes and ramifications of the Brexit vote were no easy matter for the major parties to contend with. The Conservatives, Labour and the Liberal Democrats all attempted, in various ways, to appeal to what they considered to be a simple binary logic within the electorate and use it to their electoral advantage. For the opposition parties, this proved ultimately disastrous in the UK general election of December 2019. To understand the complexities of contemporary populism, the present analysis looks back to the origins of modern democracy in the UK as that polity was the earliest and most profoundly shaped by the forces of industrial capitalism.

In Chapter 1, I begin the analysis of populism by outlining and defending a certain conception of democracy. This does not involve a typology of forms of democracy – direct as opposed to representative democracy, and so forth – but rather delineates what I consider the animating principle and, to some extent, paradox of democracy, namely popular sovereignty. Here the theory is largely drawn from two sources: on the one hand, from the democratic theory of Ernesto Laclau (2005) and Chantal Mouffe (2000) and, on the other, from the political philosophy of Jacques Rancière (2006). While there are important differences between these thinkers, the crucial commonality is an idea of democratic politics as based on radical dissent that constantly contests given political legitimacy. What Rancière, in particular, highlights is the inherent tension within any democratic polity between the bureaucratic managers and the enfranchised electorate. The former project a 'born to rule' sense of entitled social and technocratically grounded political legitimacy, while the latter contest this privilege in the name of no qualification other than their being present within the political community. This latter claim on behalf of an 'unqualified' electorate lies at the heart of the intersection between constitutional democracy and populism. On this basis, it is argued that populism is an inalienable feature of democracy and not an extraneous element bent on its destruction. In other words, populism is construed as essential rather than alien to democracy.

Having invoked 'the people' as the inalienable source of legitimacy in democracy, Chapter 2 offers a snapshot of the politics of the British workers' movements in the nineteenth century. This is the context, arguably, in which the modern democratic conception of 'the people' is constructed. E. P. Thompson's *The Making of the English Working Class*, first published in 1963, is pivotal to this chapter. It is here that a theory of class as concrete collective experience rather than statistical generalization is set out. Rehabilitating class is a crucial, though no doubt contestable, aspect of the analysis of populism offered in this book. In broad terms, the conceptualization of class offered here is 'cultural' rather than 'economic' in origins and nature. I place the two terms in scare quotes to indicate scepticism about this divide. At Eatwell and Goodwin remark of this division with regard to current understandings of populism, 'this binary debate is extremely unhelpful: real life never really works like this' (2018: 8). On the idea of working-class identity, I eschew both essentialist and statistical definitions and align my thinking with Thompson's celebrated concept of class not 'as a "structure", nor even as a "category", but as something that in fact happens (and can be shown to have happened) in human relationships' (1968: 9). This perspective allows me to reconstruct the struggles for universal enfranchisement in nineteenth-century Britain as historically constituting the linkages between democracy, working-class identity and populism.

Chapter 3 turns to the founding figures and works of British cultural studies, in which a renewed conceptualization of the working class was achieved. Richard Hoggart's *The Uses of Literacy*, published in 1957, blazed a trail in the academic portrayal of British working-class culture. This analysis highlights the very feature commonly identified as the hallmark of the populist collective consciousness: an unremitting and radical polarization between the 'Them' of the political establishment and the 'Us' of the working-class populace. Hoggart's 1950s analysis also foresaw the danger of a creeping capitalist commercialization of the British working-class lifeworld, particularly through the workings of the popular mass media.

His contemporary, and fellow cultural studies pioneer, Raymond Williams (1961), complements and amplifies this analysis with his idea of democratic popular culture as a 'long revolution'. It is the revolution of popular control over the material conditions of everyday life that constitutes Williams's notion of progressive democracy, an idea I adopt and apply to contemporary populism throughout this book. With the advent of Thatcherite neoliberalism in the UK, this revolution is stalled as the idea of collective responsibility and the practices of working-class solidarity are denigrated and steadily eroded.

Chapter 4 shows how Owen Jones's (2011) book *Chavs* documents this denigration and, in so doing, accounts for the rise of populist sentiment among the British working class. In popular news and entertainment media – amidst a landscape of exponential corporate consolidation – portrayals of the working class are transformed from a celebration of integrity in the face of adversity typical of the 1950s 'kitchen-sink drama', to a lampooning of feckless social welfare dependency and antisocial behaviour by the 1990s and beyond.

Complementing Jones's account of the denigration of working-class lives, Richard Sennett (2006, 2008, 2012) incisively portrays the demoralizing impact of neoliberal conditions of work. Most recently, these conditions have come to attention under the banner of the 'gig economy'. While this economy is defended by the executives of disruptive start-ups in the name of corporate flexibility and employee choice, the stark reality of precarious employment readily undermines this rationalizing of employment casualization and worker precarity. In this connection, Angela McRobbie's (2016) probing analysis of the 'creative industries' offers a further, devastating critique of the New Labour project. Contemporary work conditions offer thereby a powerful and concrete context in which the seeding ground of contemporary populism can be located.

Having charted the background and growth of British populism from nineteenth-century worker agitation to discontent with the gig economy of the 2010s, Chapter 5 offers a concluding prognosis of the possible future of UK liberal democracy in the wake of Brexit-based populism. Bringing together the two threads of cultural denigration and economic marginalization of the working class, the question arises: how can contemporary populism be channelled into a renewal of democratic political culture? Here I consider the complex and influential interventions of Srnicek and Williams (2016) and Mason (2015), which have in common the notion that the current wave of automation sweeping through the global economy has the potential to lead us out of the prevailing pattern of mass material scarcity and deprivation.

One of the mechanisms seen as pivotal to such a transition is a radical and scalable programme of universal basic income (UBI). I reject this solution as untenable, in part because it represents an extension of André Gorz's (2012) earlier and, I contend, implausible argument that the very idea of the 'working class' should be abandoned as automating technology and structural unemployment make work a less politically significant reality. While leftist commentators and theorists may criticize the legacy of Marxism for enthroning a 'labour theory of value', the lived reality of the working class cannot be so easily severed from its connections to socially meaningful work. In other words, progressive populism cannot, I contend, take the form of a world beyond work.

The rejection of the path set out by those who defend a worklessness-through-automation thesis leaves us essentially with one remaining route to a progressive populism. This is the reorganization of work and the economy in line with actual social value. While this may appear to many as a rather quaint conclusion, I believe it is ultimately more plausible than those antidotes to contemporary populism that see it largely as a matter of straightforward 'false consciousness' and ideological self-oppression.

As I write, in the midst of the global COVID-19 crisis in 2020, it would seem that the collective desire for social solidarity amidst the disintegrating logics of neoliberal global economics has never been more acutely felt. Who knows how this exogenous shock to the worldwide political conjuncture will play out as the current decade unfolds? One thing has already emerged which, at the start of 2020, still seemed a radical impossibility: namely, that state intervention in the global economy could be so radical, extensive and irreversible. With the neoliberal idol of the small state shattered, we may stand before a unique opportunity to channel the energy of populism towards a radical and lasting rebirth of democratic culture.

1

Populism and popular sovereignty: paradoxes of democracy

The rise of populism

In 2016, with the UK's Brexit referendum result and the election of Donald Trump as US president, media and academic attention was turned towards the phenomenon of populism with a hitherto unprecedented sense of urgency. One of the key questions that emerged was whether the tectonics of liberal democracy were shifting in some fundamental, historic way. In order to respond to this question, a necessary preliminary step is to provide a sufficiently nuanced account of what is being captured by the term 'populism'. While recent assessments of contemporary populism – such as the one offered by Eatwell and Goodwin (2018) – rest their argument on statistical evidence of voting patterns, the approach pursued here is largely the conceptual one of philosophically informed political theory. While the obvious disadvantage of such a methodology is its speculative nature, its advantage, arguably, is that it becomes possible to penetrate through to something more fundamental about the object of investigation.

While the majority of academic studies, and media accounts a fortiori, consider populism through a short-term lens of the last ten or twenty years, in this book I consider it through a much longer time frame. This will involve, in the following chapter, recounting certain elements of the British nineteenth-century workers' movements. But before any historical reconstruction of the historic origins of populism can be attempted, preliminary reflection on its nature is necessary.

The first, and obvious, thing to say is that populism is a contested concept. As indicated in the introduction, the general trend in academic treatments is to see it as a recrudescence of far-right ideology, including extreme forms of nativist nationalism. In their impressively synoptic assessment of 'national populism', Eatwell and Goodwin (2018: 5–6) identify what they call the 'Four Ds' that distinguish this phenomenon: distrust of politicians, destruction of national historical identity, deprivation due to relative inequality, and de-alignment between traditional mainstream parties and the people.

Of these four features of populism, the analysis offered in this book will lay stress mostly on the last, somewhat on the first and third, and hardly at all on the second.

The underlying reason for emphasizing the disjunction between party and people derives from the nature of party-political democracy. The people in a liberal, representative democracy articulate their preferences through a choice between parties. In 'first past the post' voting systems in nations such as the UK and US, this has historically come down to expressing a preference for one of two dominant parties. Since the early 1980s, as neoliberal political common sense has become hegemonic, a drift towards centrism has led to widespread cynicism and disenchantment with democratic party politics. Following the 2008 global financial crisis, this tendency towards popular political disenchantment has increasingly manifested itself in large-scale voting success for non-traditional parties or politicians. The appeal here is often more rhetorical than real in terms of bringing about deep social and political change. Nevertheless, the overall loss in faith in mainstream political parties is, I believe, a fundamental hallmark of contemporary populism.

To distinguish the approach to populism adopted here from another, well-established authority in this area, consider the definition of populism offered by Mudde and Kaltwasser (2012). Populism, they assert, should be understood as 'a thin-centred ideology that considers society to be ultimately separated into two homogeneous and antagonistic groups, "the pure people" and "the corrupt elite," and which argues that politics should be an expression of the volonté générale (general will) of the People' (2012: 8). What this definition misses, and is crucial to the analysis offered here, is the relationship between 'the people' and liberal democratic party politics. Political parties mediate the relationship between the state and the people.

Further, Mudde and Kaltwasser, while granting some validity to the idea of progressive populism defended by Laclau and Mouffe (considered in detail below), insist that their notion of radical democracy is 'not a viable concept' and 'lacks a clear definition' (2012: 15). This assessment stems from the fact that Mudde and Kaltwasser believe that, at the conceptual level, populism may or may not strengthen democratic political culture. While recognizing this, the analysis offered in this book seeks to draw out precisely the potential of populism to realize democracy as something 'radical', namely as the *generalized capacity on the part of the populace to determine their own material conditions of everyday existence.*

The growth of populism raises the question to what extent the disenchantment with mainstream party politics is a rejection of democratic politics in general. For those analyses of populism that accentuate links with far-right xenophobic nationalism, the answer to this question is that populism entails a desire to do away with democratic politics in favour of authoritarianism. In contrast to this dominant trend, the underlying thesis of the current analysis is the following: populism gives voice to a desire to renew the connection between liberal democratic party politics and the people. Otherwise stated: populism has arisen precisely to bring the systemic rift between the political class (including the party apparatus) and the people (primarily, the working class) into the centre of political consciousness and debate.

It follows from this thesis that populism and democracy are not to be considered incompatible or alien with respect to each other. Nor, however, does it suffice to point, in the words of Mudde and Kaltwasser (2012: 205), to 'the ambivalent relationship between populism and democracy'. Admittedly, the approach adopted to populism in this book is predicated on a certain understanding of contemporary British politics. Rather than maintaining a properly academic neutrality on populism, the analysis offered here is directed by the strong intuition that it functions as a necessary corrective to a sclerotic democratic party-political apparatus, whose highly stage-managed media appearances seem ever more distant from working-class lives.

It is also necessary to admit that, as I indicated in the introduction, there is a personal motivation to my making this argument. Coming of age in the northwest of England in the midst of Margaret Thatcher's succession of Conservative governments, it was striking to me how complacent and patronizing Conservative politicians were in the face of the decaying post-industrial landscapes that translated into interminable bleakness and depression for the population of northern England. Leaving school in 1986 at the age of sixteen, I was told by a school employment counsellor that I may as well stay in education as 'there's nothing else out there for you'. This book, then, in a certain way repays a debt to an educational system that provided me with a way out of social and economic uselessness.

The makeover of the Labour Party as 'New Labour' under Tony Blair a decade later may have, in the short term at least, made the party more electable. But the three terms of office enjoyed by Labour from 1997 to 2010 seem to have come at the very high price of driving a wedge between the party and the so-called Labour heartlands in the economically deprived north of England. *Guardian* columnist John Harris (like me, born in Cheshire in 1969) captured the slow-motion collapse of working-class support for Labour immediately following Labour's 2019 general election defeat: 'This struggle is borne out in Labour's falling vote share over 20 years: in Tony Blair's former seat of Sedgefield, in County Durham, a 71% figure in 1997 was followed by 65% in 2001, then 59% four years later, and 45% in 2010. On Thursday, when the Tories took the seat, it had fallen to 36%' (Harris, 2019).

In the face of such a decline in vote share in the Labour heartlands, the question is why working-class voters shifted their allegiance to what they largely still recognize as their historical enemy, the Conservative Party. Just before the 2019 UK general election, Harris reflected on his decade-long video project investigating popular opinion in places peripheral to the UK media-sphere, *Anywhere but Westminster*. In a long-form piece for the *Guardian* (Harris and Domokos, 2019), he remarked: 'Lots of analysis and data since that referendum has cast doubt on the idea that Brexit was some kind of working-class revolt. But all across Britain, in neglected places that rarely saw TV cameras, we had met people who were voting to leave the EU as a way of calling for change: to be heard.' This desire for political recognition among working-class constituents is, I argue in this book, a primary driver of contemporary populism in liberal democracies.

To make the same point in a different way, the argument advanced here is that populism registers an unsatisfied desire, primarily among working-class voters, for demonstrable democratic accountability on the part of their political representatives. What the Brexit vote and the two ensuing UK general elections in 2017 and 2019 seemed to make clear was that large swathes of the electorate were reacting to a felt lack of recognition of them and accountability towards them on the part of their political representatives. While there was only a small majority (52 per cent to 48 per cent) in favour of Britain leaving the EU in the June 2016 referendum (see Guardian, 2016), the fact that the Labour Party, under the leadership of Jeremy Corbyn between 2016 and 2019, was not prepared unambiguously to back the UK's withdrawal from the EU appears to have radically alienated it from its traditional working-class supporters. This very much played into the hands of Conservative leader Boris Johnson's simple pledge to 'get Brexit done' in the 2019 general election.

It is one thing to contend that contemporary populism is not, in essence, anti-democratic; it is quite another to demonstrate, in positive terms, how populism gives voice to a collective desire to renew democratic political culture. In common with populism itself, the very notion of democracy is highly contested. Political discourse on democracy has become mired in commonplaces about 'free and fair elections' and the 'international rule of law'. While not wishing to deny that these are important political desiderata, what is needed is a more concrete sense of democratic political community. Accordingly, I will understand 'democracy' in this book as a kind of collective lived experience, along the lines of what Raymond Williams famously termed a 'structure of feeling' (1961: 63). To flesh this out, our first task is to construct a compelling and suitably nuanced concept of democracy.

To advance my argument, therefore, in this chapter I will draw on the political theory of Ernesto Laclau, Jacques Rancière and Chantal Mouffe.

In conjunction, these thinkers mount a consistent and cogent challenge to the hegemonic liberal view of democracy as a procedural set of norms pertaining to the internationally recognized 'rule of law'. The work of Jürgen Habermas is foundational in constructing and advancing this conception of democratic politics. Habermas's notions of communicative action (1985) and discourse ethics (1990) laid the foundations for further elaborations of 'deliberative democracy' (see Gutmann and Thompson, 1996), which grasp democratic culture as governed by an overriding drive towards consensus-building and transparent agreement guided by universal norms.

By contrast, Laclau, Rancière and Mouffe view the dynamics of democratic culture through the lens of dissent and disagreement. Crucially, from the 1980s on, they also anticipated the rise of populism across liberal and social democracies as the traditional parties of the left drifted ever further from their roots in nineteenth-century socialism and the popular workers' movements. What is common to these theorists is the recognition that democracy rests on an irresolvable question about adequately representing 'the people'. For these thinkers, the notion of popular sovereignty is at once the basis for and most challenging issue of modern democratic theory.

Democracy and disagreement

Jacques Rancière is an influential contemporary French philosopher whose writings, spanning five decades, centre on issues of labour and work, society and politics, and aesthetics and knowledge. Some of his more overtly political works are *Disagreement* (1999 [1995]) and *Hatred of Democracy* (2006). In his earlier work *Proletarian Nights* (2012), published in 1981, Rancière documented and analysed in great detail the writings of nineteenth-century French artisans which expressed their dreams of economic and social emancipation. In the preface to the new English translation, Rancière notes: 'If this book goes against the current now, in an age which proclaims the disappearance of the proletariat, it should be remembered that it also did so at a time that still upheld the consistency of the working class united by the condition of the factory and the science of capitalist production' (2012: viii).

As Rancière goes on to clarify, it was the Marxist belief in worker 'false consciousness' which he sought to dispel in this his early book: that is, the idea that only an 'enlightened' working class can be politically effective. An analogous thesis guides Rancière's *The Ignorant Schoolmaster* (1991 [1987]), a study of the eighteenth-century Belgian pedagogue Joseph Jacatot, who advanced the radical idea that any learner already contains within themselves what is needed for their own self-development and emancipation.

The common thread running through Rancière's thought is that 'the people' assert their desire to be seen and heard against the constant resistance of those who deem them unqualified to speak. We can readily recognize how this idea lends itself to the treatment of populism. As noted, populism presents itself through an oppositional logic between an 'Us' of the people and a 'Them' of the established political and cultural elite. As indicated in the introduction, the dominant interpretation of this 'Us' versus 'Them' dichotomy is that it is, at base, driven by exclusive nationalism and xenophobic nativism. What Rancière's line of thinking does here is open a space within which populism can be seen, instead, as an essential dynamic within progressive democratic political culture.

In his more recent work, Rancière has tended to focus his political critique on the hypocritical denial by the liberal democratic establishment that they employ mechanisms of technocratic authoritarianism to maintain order within the political community. In Rancière's rather idiosyncratic terms, this tendency towards technocratic rule reduces 'the political' proper to a managerial form of governance he refers to as 'the police'. As Rancière puts this in *Disagreement*: 'Democracy is more precisely the name of a singular disruption of this order of distribution of bodies as a community that we proposed to conceptualize in the broader concept of the police. It is the name of what comes and interrupts the smooth working of this order through a singular mechanism of subjectification' (1999: 99).

According to Rancière's analysis, since the 1980s Western liberal democracies have become increasingly dominated by methods of 'the police', to the detriment of what he considers 'the political', this latter being considered an open-ended process of popular contestation. 'The police' and 'the political' represent for him dialectical terms held in dynamic tension rather than mutually exclusive formations of the political community. Rancière also argues that the neoliberal configuration of politics, with its attendant political theory of consensus-driven deliberative democracy, has resulted in a condition of 'postdemocracy'. Commenting on the ubiquity of opinion polls, for instance, he remarks: 'The utopia of postdemocracy is that of an uninterrupted count that presents the total of "public opinion" as identical to the body of the people' (1999: 103).

For Rancière, both in theory and in practice the emergence of modern democracy centres the permanent contestation of political power in and through 'the people'. As he notes, the history of actually existing liberal democracy can be read in terms of various protracted efforts to subvert, limit or circumvent this appeal to popular sovereignty. On Rancière's view, appeal to the popular will amounts to asserting a political principle that constantly interrupts and questions any time-honoured source of legitimacy. Further, appealing to 'the people' involves calling on nobody in particular – that is, on everyone regardless of any particular knowledge or other qualification. A populist conception of democratic politics thereby emerges in opposition to the managerial 'business as usual' mode whereby the only valid voices are possessed by individuals demonstrating sufficient social, cultural and economic capital. As Rancière (2016) succinctly puts in a short essay: '[Populism] is a certain attitude of rejection in relationship to prevailing governmental practices' (2016: 101).

For Rancière, typical portrayals of contemporary populism draw on well-rehearsed and culturally established tropes of 'the people' as a mob tending to unleash unthinking violence on cultivated civil society and intolerant of anyone and anything seen as other. He thereby makes clear how the hegemonic reaction to populism in liberal democracies summons up 'an image of the people developed at the end of the nineteenth century by thinkers like Hippolyte Taine and Gustave Le Bon, frightened by the Commune of Paris and the rise of the workers' movement' (2016: 103). As for the reflexive condemnation of populist xenophobia, Rancière lambasts proponents of seemingly benign managerial liberal democracy who claim they are defending fairness and openness when in fact they are managing the entry and conditions of 'resident aliens' in the name of economic expediency: 'there is a whole panoply of state measures: restricted entry to the country; refusal to give papers to those who have worked, participated, and paid taxes in France for years; restrictions on the right of birthplace; double penalty; laws against the foulard and burqa; imposed numbers of border escorts; breaking up nomadic camps' (2016: 103).

Rancière's (2006) understanding of democratic political culture is fundamentally opposed to what he considers a reduction of politics to ethics along the lines set out in Habermas's political theory: 'Consensus is the reduction of these different ways of being the "people" into a single one, one that is identical with the counting of the population and of its parts, and with the counting of the interests of the global community and of its parts' (2007: 32). Here, Rancière has in mind Habermas's influential model of 'discourse ethics', which conceives of democratic culture as governed by a regulative ideal of transparent discussion and consensus-building among those affected by a decision-making process. Habermas identifies three conditions of such morally regulated democratic discourse: '(1) all have the same chances to initiate speech acts, to question, to interrogate, and to open debate; (2) all have the same right to question the assigned topics of conversation; and (3) all have the same right to initiate reflexive arguments about the very rules of the discourse procedure and the way in which they are applied' (Benhabib, 1996: 70).

Rancière rejects what he sees as Habermas's reduction or subordination of politics to ethics: 'Ethics amounts to the dissolution of the norm into the fact – the identification of all forms of discourse and practice under the same indistinct point of view' (2007: 28). What informs Rancière's critique of Habermasian discourse ethics and deliberative democracy is an overriding suspicion that it serves as a theoretical justification for neoliberal conservatism. By contrast, Rancière views the essential dynamism of democratic political culture as a matter of challenging rather than legitimating established power. What we find opposed here are radically different viewpoints on the very nature of the democratic political community:

> [Consensus] signifies a mode of symbolic structuration of the community that empties out the political core that constitutes it, namely dissension. A political community is indeed a community that is structurally divided, not divided between diverging interest groups and opinions, but divided in relation to itself. A political 'people' is never the same thing as the sum of a population. (Rancière, 2007: 31–2)

Looking back over a distance of two decades to his book *The Philosopher and His Poor*, originally published in 1983, Rancière captures the appearance of 'the people' that constitutes democracy in terms of being able to enter public space outside of work time: 'The *demos* is the collection of workers insofar as they have the time to do something other than their work and to find themselves in another place than that of its performance' (2004: 226). Simply put, the advent of democracy involves workers not knowing their place or, at least, not sticking to it. This offers an account of the democratic condition clearly at odds with that of managerial technocracy, where something is given to the people as more or less passive recipients. The people here are heard only as the child is typically heard, by someone competent to know what the child cannot. Authoritarian populism works on the same principle, where the charismatic demagogue ardently proclaims his identity with the will of 'the people'. Giving the initiative, in terms of political praxis, to the electorate is as unwanted by such populism as it is by its mainstream liberal democratic opponents.

What Rancière's political thinking allows us to do is to avoid any identification of such authoritarian populism with populism simpliciter. The central contention being advanced here is that contemporary populism does not represent something inimical to democratic political culture but rather something essential to it. In Rancière's thinking, democracy amounts to an interruption of a social-political equation according to which legitimate political rule puts everyone in their right place. Democratic politics, on his understanding, interrupts this assumed pre-established harmony but offers, in turn, no given formula for predetermining who has the right to rule.

This democratic interruption stems from a basic appeal to equality – but not equality in the sense of statistically calibrated social welfare conditions, share of wealth and income and so forth. Rather, the democratic drive for equality takes the form of a demand that anyone and everyone counts, regardless of qualification. Rancière's afterword to *The Philosopher and His Poor* sums this up succinctly and powerfully: 'The *demos* that gives [democracy] its name is neither the ideal people of sovereignty, nor the sum of the parties of this society. It is properly a supplement to any "realist" account of social parties. In the natural history of the forms of domination, only this supplement can bring forth democratic exceptionality' (2004: 225).

In the most direct account of his theoretical position, *Hatred of Democracy* (2006), Rancière insists that all actually existing democracies amount to more or less liberal oligarchies. This is not, in itself, a crucial point, as he accepts that any democracy must in reality take on some form of oligarchic rule. But he now discerns an almost completed collapse of the democratic egalitarian demand under the weight of a combined oligarchy of state bureaucracy and global commerce: 'we are no longer in an age of expert juridical constructions designed to inscribe the irreducible "power of the people" in oligarchic constitutions. This figure of the political and of political science is behind us. State power and the power of wealth tendentially unite in a sole expert management of monetary and population flows' (2006: 95).

While Rancière is clearly articulating an increasingly acute attenuation of properly democratic culture, he stops short of announcing its definitive demise. Instead, in the final words of *Hatred of Democracy*, he presents the democratic ideal as a key object of desire or fear within the political field: '[Democracy] is not borne along by any historical necessity and does not bear any. It is only entrusted to the constancy of its specific acts. This can provoke fear, and so hatred, among those who are used to exercising the magisterium of thought. But among those who know how to share with anybody and everybody the equal power of intelligence, it can conversely inspire courage, and hence joy' (2006: 97). Thus, while we are not witnessing the end of the democratic spirit under the conditions of advanced neoliberalism, according to Rancière: 'The thesis of the new hatred of democracy can be succinctly put: there is only one good democracy, the one that represses the catastrophe of democratic civilization' (2006: 4). As he is well aware, however, the cultural critique of democracy runs parallel to its modern emergence.

In this book, I will reconstruct this criticism of democratic culture in Chapter 3, largely from a British perspective, when considering the work of Raymond Williams. In *Culture and Society* (1958) Williams identifies such a critique starting with Edmund Burke in the late eighteenth century and continuing, through Romanticism, to the high Victorian period with John Ruskin, Matthew Arnold and John Stuart Mill. What united these political thinkers and social commentators was a conviction that the rise of democratic culture was levelling out or even destroying individual intellectual and moral excellence. Their earlier 'hatred of democracy' comes in the form of a fear that the industrial working class, rendered morally vicious through their conditions of work, would spontaneous rise up against their social and political masters.

Hence their urgent desire to promote education and culture as a means of social pacification. Only when the masses had been sufficiently improved by such means could they be trusted with the vote and other endowments of genuine moral autonomy. Against this backdrop, of course, any form of insurrectionary social revolution was the one thing to be avoided at all cost. The rule of the demos might be acknowledged as a condition suitable to the distant future, but it was by no means to be brought about while the moral condition of the average worker remained so abject.

Whereas Marx endowed the industrial proletariat with the historically defined agency to bring about the social revolution needed to annul the contradictions of bourgeois capitalism, Rancière distances himself from any determinate social nature of democratic agency. He insists the problem is not one of representative versus 'direct' democracy, because this takes democracy to be a matter of 'juridical-political forms'. For Rancière, it is not a type of constitution, parliamentary system or extension of the franchise that identifies democracy: 'Democracy has no natural consequences precisely because it is the division of "nature", the breaking of the link between natural properties and forms of government' (2006: 54). As he puts it even more sharply: 'There is, strictly speaking, no such thing as democratic government. Government is always exercised by the minority over the majority. The "power of the people" is ... what separates the exercise of government from the representation of society' (p. 52). This amounts to saying that democracy is the manner in which society resists its subjugation to government. In his earlier language, it is an affirmation of 'politics' against 'the police'.

In his political theory Rancière offers us a concept of democracy as contested political legitimacy in the name of radical, qualitatively conceived equality. In so doing, he opens a space for a non-authoritarian and genuinely progressive populism. Recognizing such a populism allows us to question the hegemonic interpretations of contemporary populism as inherently authoritarian and regressive. When populism is so reduced, this blocks the possibility of seeing it as a catalyst for democratic renewal, a renewal urgently required in light of the systemic and manifest social, political and ecological failings of contemporary neoliberal governance. In order to construct a compelling and effective critique of neoliberalism, populism must be seen as a potential source of renewal within the heart of contemporary liberal democracy.

Democracy and the demos

The Argentinian political theorist Ernesto Laclau offers a critique of democratic managerialism that has many obvious affinities with Rancière's condemnation of a decades-long slide into authoritarian technocracy on the part of liberal democracies. Like Rancière, Laclau is interested in reconceptualizing and rehabilitating the notion of 'the people' in the context of democratic political culture. Common to both thinkers is also an effort to eschew any simplistic reformulation of working-class identity and agency along the lines of an orthodox Marxist understanding of the historical role of the proletariat. Turning now to Laclau will allow us to develop, in more explicit detail, the idea of progressive populism as a renewal of democratic political culture.

According to Laclau, it is noteworthy that populism is generally seen by democratic theorists and practitioners alike as a regression and degeneration in democratic political culture: 'From the very beginning, a strong element of ethical condemnation has been present in the consideration of populist movements. Populism has not only been demoted: it has also been denigrated' (Laclau, 2005: 19). Just as Rancière alludes to a long-standing suspicion of the mass psychology of crowds in instances such as the Paris Commune of 1871, Laclau connects the rejection of populism to a legacy of conservative critique relating to all insurrectionary political movements. Laclau's defence of populism does not stem from any sentimentalized notion of 'the people' fighting faceless forces of oppressive power, but it does insist that the fundamental driver of democratic political culture is organized opposition and dissent with respect to the political status quo.

While he recognizes that there can be no question of essentializing 'the people' or resurrecting one-dimensional representations of the proletariat, Laclau is equally adamant that reference to 'the people' should not be rendered taboo within democratic discourse for fear of evoking ghosts of chauvinist or even fascist political sentiments. As he puts it: 'The construction of a "people" is the *sine qua non* of democratic functioning. Without production of emptiness there is no "people", no populism, but no democracy either' (2005: 169). In other words, populism is an intrinsic feature of democratic political culture. By 'emptiness' Laclau means a certain radical indeterminacy in relation to 'the people' as political subject, as opposed to regressive forms of populism where 'the people' is readily determined in exclusive ethno-racial terms. Similarly, central to the argument advanced in this book is the recognition that 'the people' can perform the role of constituting a progressive democratic politics free of the essentializing xenophobia all too apparent in right-wing populist movements and parties.

Laclau's analysis of the political signification of 'the people' is derived from his understanding of Jacques Lacan's (2006 [1966]) theory of signs and symbolization. Exploring Lacan's theory in detail in the present context would draw us too far away from our basic task of constructing a cogent theory of populism. The key point is that, following his interpretation of Lacan's theory of the symbolic, Laclau grasps the meaning of 'the people' not as a substantial, essentialized subject but rather as something constituted through political demands. It follows from this that 'the people' cannot be reduced to determinate markers of national belonging, such as one finds in nativist, reactionary populism. The kind of populism Laclau has in mind, therefore, constitutes a political community not in terms of a common identity but rather thanks to overlapping and interlocking demands. In other words, referring democratic rule back to 'the people' does not entail any recourse to an essentialized national subject in the manner seen in regressive, authoritarian populism.

As Laclau and Mouffe's *Hegemony and Socialist Strategy* (2005 [1985]) puts it: 'The "people" as the articulating instance – the locus of what we have called popular demands – can result only from the hegemonic overdetermination of a particular democratic demand which functions, as we have explained, as an empty signifier (as an *objet petit a* in the Lacanian sense)' (Laclau and Mouffe, 2005: 127). Politics, on this Lacanian rendering, is not practised in the name of a pre-existing common subject called 'the people', which makes demands within a political system. Rather, it is the formulation of the demand that constitutes 'the people' as a political subject in the first place. Accordingly, such 'populism' would name the practical understanding of the political that seeks to constitute 'the people' through the articulation of common demands.

If populism can be understood in such democratic terms, what is it that gives rise to the generalized condemnation of contemporary populism? In answer to this question Laclau (2005) cites Gustave Le Bon's book *Psychology of Crowds* (2009), first published in 1895, as a key exhibit. The notion central to Le Bon's social theory is that the assemblage of the crowd and consequent constitution of mass psychology represents significant cultural regression. Laclau quotes the following passage from Le Bon's nineteenth-century analysis: 'by the mere fact that he forms part of an organised crowd, a man descends several rungs in the ladder of civilization. Isolated, he may be a cultivated individual; in a crowd, he is a barbarian – that is, a creature acting by instinct' (2005: 29). According to Le Bon, crowd psychology amounts to a pathological contagion of unreason.

According to Laclau, Le Bon's moralizing critique of crowd psychology gives voice to a dominant suspicion of mass popular action as degenerate and regressive. This then sets the stage for all subsequent treatments of democratic populism. It is essential to see the inherent paternalism written into this critique. Through its lens, populism is seen in terms of 'the people' demanding what is not good for them, as defined by a political, academic and cultural establishment who apparently know better. And this incapacity and illegitimacy of 'the people' involved in collective action is seen as a natural consequence of democracy approximating too closely to the rule of the people – that is, its approximating to genuine democracy!

In the conclusion of *On Populist Reason*, Laclau underscores 'the *constitutive* role that we have attributed to social *heterogeneity*' (2005: 223). This means that progressive populism never rests on the configuration of a unified people as such, but rather takes the form of relatively fluid demands. Thus, 'the people' 'designates not a *given* group, but an act of institution that creates a new agency out of a plurality of heterogeneous elements' (p. 224). Right-wing populism, by contrast, rests on the construction of a radically homogeneous 'people', the qualifications of which can become, arbitrarily, more exclusive over time.

Finally, Laclau also notes the closeness of his own theory of populism to Rancière's political philosophy as sketched out above. He notes: 'Rancière's notion of a class that is not a class, that has as a particular determination something in the nature of a universal exclusion ... is not far from what I have called "emptiness"' (2005: 246). The key commonality between the two thinkers alluded to here is that of the radical heterogeneity of 'the people'. The actual administration of liberal democracy works constantly to overcome this indeterminacy of legitimate democratic agency, by recognizing more or less exclusive features of a 'legitimate' electorate. But the history of struggles for popular enfranchisement is essentially a struggle to cancel selective qualifications: property qualifications, educational qualifications, age qualification, gender qualifications and so forth. These are, simply put, ways of determining the part of the people who count as opposed to those who do not count for political purposes. In progressive populism, such markers of legitimacy give way to the formulation of common demands by 'the people', namely those who count regardless of qualification.

While the analysis presented in this book follows the spirit of Laclau's defence of progressive populism, it is important also to note a certain distance from the letter of his theory. In later chapters of this book, the focus is on a reconstruction of *working-class* progressive politics. This makes the approach here, broadly speaking, a Marxian one. As Mudde and Kaltwasser note, Laclau develops a concept of populism where it 'is understood as a particular political logic, not as the result of particular class alliances' (2012: 6). Problematizing what was considered an overly deterministic Marxist notion of historic class agency is, of course, a stock in trade of the New Left more generally.

Any detailed consideration of the multifarious critiques of the Marxist construction of class goes far beyond the scope of this book. What can be said, however, is that Laclau's recourse to the Lacanian idea of 'empty signifier' to capture the demands of populist politics risks making political agency excessively fluid and indeterminate. As Mudde and Kaltwasser remark, 'Laclau's theory of populism is, on the one hand, extremely abstract, and on the other hand, it proposes a concept of populism that becomes so vague and malleable it loses much of its analytic utility' (2012: 7). Thus, it is important to note that Laclau's theory of populism is outlined at the beginning of the current analysis to indicate only a point of departure. Beyond this first chapter, the underlying task will be to concretize the direction of travel indicated by this initial construction of populism by means of a reconstruction of British working-class politics.

Mouffe and the democratic paradox

The last theorist to be analysed in this chapter is Chantal Mouffe. Mouffe, a Belgian political theorist based in the UK for many years, was married to Laclau from 1975 until his death in 2014 and shares much of his theory of democracy. While broadly in agreement with the notion of progressive populism advanced by Rancière and Laclau, Mouffe's central concern is the fate of leftist politics during the era of the rise in neoliberalism and following the collapse of the Soviet Union in the 1980s. In more direct and explicit terms than the other two thinkers, Mouffe spells out how the severing of the ties between the legacy of the socialist workers' movements and leftist party politics in Europe has rendered the democratic party system incapable of opposing the common sense of hegemonic neoliberal governance.

More specifically, Mouffe's political analysis centres on the transformation of traditional leftist parties into consensus-based centre-left parties that seek to do politics in a spirit that proclaims the end of left/right political divisions. This centrist makeover, Mouffe argues, has removed the essential dynamic element of liberal democracies, namely a credible choice between truly distinct political visions and platforms. As the mainstream political spectrum becomes narrower, she contends, the democratic electorate becomes increasingly frustrated with the political class, who now appear 'all the same'. The result is that voters become easy prey for a recrudescence of extremism, particularly right-wing xenophobic nationalism, which is able to offer psychological compensation for widespread disenchantment with the political class.

In *The Democratic Paradox* (2000), Mouffe situates this process explicitly in the context of a triumphant neoliberalism: 'Neo-liberal dogmas about the inviolable rights of property, the all-encompassing virtues of the market and the dangers of interfering with its logics constitute nowadays the "common sense" in liberal-democratic societies and they are having a profound impact on the left, as many left parties are moving to the right and euphemistically redefining themselves as "centre-left"' (2000: 6). In conjunction with this assessment of the health of liberal democracy party politics, Mouffe offers an examination of the political theorists John Rawls and Jürgen Habermas, who both seek to reconcile liberalism and democracy. For these thinkers, she contends, this reconciliation comes down to a balancing act between the claims of individual liberty and those of social equality.

We have seen how Rancière grasps the egalitarian spirit as the key element underlying democratic culture. The concern for individual liberty, albeit seen through a particular, arguably narrowing lens, is central to neoliberalism. Both Rawls and Habermas, Mouffe argues, resolve the problem of how to reconcile liberalism and democracy by appealing to ideals of rational consensus: Rawls (1999) through the thought experiment of an original social contract arrived at under a 'veil of ignorance'; Habermas (1990) by the normative power of an 'ideal speech situation'.

This appeal to consensus as something undergirding democracy is precisely what Mouffe contests. For her, democratic politics is all about interminable, but principled *dis*agreement. This doesn't mean things won't get done under democratic rule, but rather that political parties need to offer genuinely distinct perspectives on the issues that matter most to the electorate. Accordingly, Mouffe (2000) labels the position she advocates 'agonistic pluralism' and argues that 'the aim of democratic politics is to transform *antagonism* into *agonism*. This requires providing channels through which collective passions will be given ways to express themselves over issues which, while allowing enough possibility for identification, will not construct the opponent as an enemy but as an adversary' (2000: 103).

In *On the Political* (2005), Mouffe extends her earlier critique of consensus-based politics and reaffirms the need for 'agonism' within democracy in the form of political parties which articulate different social visions and the need for democratic politics to mobilize collective identifications. The received wisdom she is opposing here is the sense that we have entered a post-ideological age of democracy in which the cardinal left/right distinctions are inexorably giving way to a centrism based on shared rational interests.

While the conceptual framework is essentially the same in the two books, *On the Political* reflects the real difference of political atmosphere brought about in 2001 by the 9/11 attacks and President Bush's declaration of a 'war on terror' (Bush, 2001). Mouffe recognizes that this 'war' constitutes a crucial divide, but one that is cast in the moral terms of a good free West against an 'axis of evil' (Bush, 2002).

Within European politics Mouffe notes the emergence, around the same time, of various right-wing populist parties. She singles out the Austrian Freedom Party led by Jörg Haider as particularly telling and rejects the dominant explanation, offered at the time, that this party's rise was largely due to Austria not having fully come to terms with its Nazi past. After noting the parallel developments of the Vlaams Blok in Belgium (her country of origin) and the Front National in France, Mouffe then turns her attention to the success of the UK Independence Party (UKIP) in the 2004 European Parliament election. In light of the 2016 Brexit result, Mouffe's comments from over a decade beforehand look extremely prescient: 'It is undeniable that all the conditions nowadays exist in Britain for a right-wing populist party to exploit the popular frustration. Since the move to the right of New Labour under the leadership of Tony Blair, many traditional Labour voters no longer feel represented by the party' (2005: 71).

UKIP went on to attain ever-greater visibility and support under the leadership of Nigel Farage, initially from 2006 to 2009 and then later from 2010 to 2016. In 2013, UKIP gained 25 per cent overall in UK local elections (Sparrow and Neild, 2013) and was, by then, clearly a force to be reckoned with. Given these subsequent developments, Mouffe's warning of the danger of regressive populism arising where the traditionally dominant parties fail to articulate distinct political needs and demands was convincingly corroborated. Equally, however, it is important not to misinterpret the rise of UKIP as solely driven by resentment politics on the part of an increasingly marginalized and aging constituency. As Eatwell and Goodwin caustically insist: 'Simply to dismiss national-populist movements as a final resting place for old men is incredibly misleading' (2018: 27–8).

Drawing on the work of the Weimar-period political theorist Carl Schmitt (2005 [1922]), Mouffe recognizes what she refers to as 'the democratic paradox'. This consists in the tension (Schmitt insisted on the stronger notion of irreconcilability) of the liberal appeal to a universalist rights-based equality and the democratic ideal of a people's self-governance. Mouffe sees 'this constitutive paradox' (2000: 45) as the principal challenge or problem within liberal democracy. Part of the tension here is between the methodological individualism espoused by liberalism and the collective identity projected and appealed to by the nation state.

In contemporary theoretical approaches to democracy, especially the 'deliberative democracy' paradigm founded on the work of Habermas (see Gutmann and Thompson, 1996), Mouffe identifies two specific problems. The first is a certain rationalistic bias that leads theorists to underplay or fail to recognize the key role emotions and desires clearly play in actual democratic politics. The second is the idea that the popular will can be measured by aggregating individual preferences. The point here is that the popular will cannot be reduced to an averaged preferential choice expressed by a unitary subject, 'the people'. This connects closely with the critique of Habermasian consensus-based political theory. Mouffe opposes this approach as it holds all parties to a principled disagreement to an overriding universal norm of conflict resolution. To affirm the validity of this norm is to gut liberal democracy of the very multiplicity of incompatible perspectives that grants it its political dynamism.

As with the paradox, so too this recognition of conflict at the heart of democracy is not to be definitively resolved but rather given shape. This takes the form, as we have seen, of what Mouffe refers to as 'agonistic pluralism'. The key medium of expression for such pluralism is, in turn, the political parties which grant institutional form and historical longevity to collective identities within the democratic electorate. In accounting for the rise of populism, weakened party loyalty on the part of the electorate is often cited as a key cause. It is tempting, as this disjunction between electorates becomes more pronounced, to call time on the viability of multi-party liberal democracy in general.

For Mouffe, as noted, the real democratic problem fails to come to light through this kind of analysis: namely, that a 'postdemocratic' condition has transformed parties from semi-stable collective identities into depoliticized receptacles of voter preference. It is easy to see here how the political domain is being subjected to neoliberalization, where voters become consumers of particular policies or, more typically and corrosively, political personalities. Added to the 'post-political' idea of universal consensus, the price paid by this neoliberalizing of democratic culture is an emergence of an 'outside' that escapes the logic of inter-party difference. In Mouffe's words: 'Too much emphasis on consensus and the refusal of confrontation lead to apathy and disaffection with political participation. Worse still, the result can be the crystallization of collective passions around issues which cannot be managed by the democratic process and an explosion of antagonisms that can tear up the very basis of civility' (2000: 104).

Mouffe's allusion here is to right-wing populism, which does not constitute an intra-democratic form of 'agonism', but rather generates an antagonism that takes the form of pitting 'the people' against the democratic political establishment more generally. This invocation of the collective typically results in an identity politics whereby only certain subsets of the population properly and exclusively belong to the nation state. Anti-immigrant sentiments are, almost invariably, seized upon in this construction of nativist belonging. The war on terror has rendered Islam a typical signifier for those excluded. In the face of this tendency towards right-wing populism, insists Mouffe, the aim of democratic politics 'is to transform *antagonism* into agonism' (2000: 103).

Although Mouffe rejects the paradigm of deliberative democracy, according to which democratic culture should be regulated by a universalized norm of consensus-building, she does concede that her own understanding involves a broader notion of 'conflictual consensus': 'This is indeed the privileged terrain of agonistic confrontation among adversaries' (2000: 103). In other words, democracy essentially amounts to political disagreement that remains bound to the fundamental concerns of liberty and equality. The hegemony of the neoliberal mutation of democracy, however, has resulted in an extremely attenuated field of democratic dispute where the rival models of social democracy, radical democracy and so forth are ruled out as unrealistic from the outset. In other words, there has been an alarming narrowing of political 'common sense' during the period of neoliberal ascendancy, with leftist parties drifting ever more strongly towards a centrist or even right-of-centre position.

Mouffe's (2000) analysis of the eclipse of leftist politics in the 1990s complements Rancière's diagnosis. Most explicitly in the form of 'Third Way' politics championed by Blair's New Labour project and conceptualized by Giddens (1998) as a post-Marxist reconstitution of social democratic politics, the social change invoked by leftist parties becomes a matter of consensual centrism 'beyond left and right'. As Blair stated at the Labour Party annual conference in 1999, two years into his first term of office: 'The Third Way is not a new way between progressive and conservative politics. It is progressive politics distinguishing itself from conservatism of left or right. New Labour must be the new radicals who take on both of them, not just on election day but every day' (Blair, 1999).

While the 2019 general election result was widely reported in terms of voters in Labour's traditional heartlands deserting the party, for Mouffe it is really a question of realizing that Labour deserted its traditional working-class constituency two decades earlier. More generally, Mouffe claims that parallel developments within the party politics of European liberal democracies were the main cause of a recrudescence of extreme right nationalism and, ultimately, regressive populism, across a supposedly post-ideological Europe. Accordingly, the neoliberalization of the state led to a collapse of traditional working-class parties into a virtually unquestioned common sense of free-market centrism, thereby leaving working-class voters with no effective outlets for their demands.

It is, then, within this eclipse of genuine working-class party representation, rather than in any generalized disaffection with liberal democratic politics, that the proximate cause of the rise of populism is to be sought. With this diagnosis goes the complementary solution of reconstituting cogent and effective leftist parties that, once again, perform the task of recognizing and acting on the demands of the working-class electorate. This, I wish to argue here, is the real message of contemporary populism: the need for a reformulation of leftist party politics that meets the demands of a working-class electorate subjected, over the last four decades, to the rigours of unrelenting neoliberal governance.

Conclusion

Examining the democratic theories of Rancière, Laclau and Mouffe has allowed us to gain a clear conceptual understanding of the place of populism within contemporary liberal democracy. Rancière grasps the idea of popular sovereignty in terms of a demand to be counted regardless of one's competency in the eyes of the bureaucratic powers that oversee and administer any actually existing democracy. For Laclau, similarly, the central problem is reaching an adequate understanding of 'the people', not as an essential substance, but rather as a fluid political agency generated by concrete demands. Finally, Mouffe underscores the need for a vibrant culture of democratic party-political pluralism and difference. All three thinkers are united by a common effort to make sense of the fate of leftist democratic politics in light of the neoliberal political common sense installed since the early 1980s.

The main reason for choosing these theorists for beginning the analysis of populism offered here is that they situate the crisis of democracy on a common ground: the collapse of party-political dynamics into a managerial technocracy presided over by a centrist political class. The programme of neoliberal governance that has constituted political reality over the last four decades was always conceived and presented as a kind of counter-revolutionary movement (see Harvey, 2005). Of particular concern to neoliberal ideologues such as Milton Friedman was the role of labour unions in national politics (see Friedman and Friedman, 1990: 228–47). Severing the working-class vote from party representation informed by union perspectives and power thus emerged as a key desideratum in the neoliberal transition. Rendering the working class politically homeless has allowed regressive populism to emerge. But the point here is to see the possibility of reformulating progressive party politics by redirecting the current of present populist sentiment.

The key thing, then, is not to reject populism *in toto* in the face of the current wave of regressive populism. The argument made in this book is that the populist sentiment is, in general terms, meaningful and necessary.

The work that needs to be done is to reform leftist party politics so that the populist sentiment is channelled into and articulated by genuinely progressive leftist political parties. That requires, in the context of UK politics, a new 'New Labour', namely a party that shapes a politics that responds to twenty-first-century working and social conditions, just as the nineteenth- and twentieth-century socialist movements attempted to do in the face of the very different conditions of industrial capitalism.

What has been lost along the way to regressive populism is not simply the political power of labour but a shared historical consciousness of the nature and purpose of democracy. Accordingly, having begun with a chapter which offers a theoretical clarification of the relationship between populism and democracy, the next chapter looks back to a seminal instance of a nineteenth-century organized workers' movement: the British Reform Movement from the 1820s to the 1870s. During this period, the world's leading capitalist country was confronted with a generations-long struggle to recognize the political legitimacy of common working men.

The eventual victories of this struggle include many of the stock features of any progressive society: generalized enfranchisement, guaranteed conditions of work, legalized union representation and (albeit limited) state-funded education. By examining the history of the social movements that advanced these causes we can regain a solid footing with regard to the key social stakes involved in democratic political struggle. What will emerge from this historical reconstruction in the next chapter is that the mass mobilization of working-class political praxis was instrumental in bringing about the modern liberal democratic nation state as we know it. The basic lesson to be learnt here is that 'the popular will' was not exhausted and surpassed in this foundational stage of modern democracy. On the contrary, a resurgence of progressive populism is necessary if liberal democracy is not to decay further into a binary choice between neoliberal technocracy and increasingly authoritarian nativist nationalism.

2

Democracy and the working class

The preceding chapter offered an initial analysis of populism as something not only consistent with but intrinsic to democratic culture. As I will argue in this chapter, the origins of democratic political culture reside in protracted working-class struggle in the late eighteenth and nineteenth centuries. The conception of class adopted here will be a relational one. As Ellen Meiksins Wood (2016) notes, there are, broadly speaking, two paradigms of analysis, according to which class is considered 'as a structural *location* or as a social *relation*' (2016: 76). Wood elaborates on the relational definition as follows: 'Class enters the picture ... when some people are systematically compelled by differential access to the means of production or appropriation to transfer surplus labour to others' (p. 108). The fundamental *experience* of the working class is thereby characterized by generalized exploitation and lack of material autonomy. The advance of popular democratic reform is, in class terms, a countermove designed to overcome, by degrees, this condition of exploitative dependency. This includes but is by no means limited to broadening the franchise.

With respect to contemporary populism, there are two basic factors motivating my assertion of the intrinsic connection between democracy and working-class struggle. First, the widespread assumption that populism is fundamentally anti-democratic in spirit. This assumption is based, I believe, on a misreading of the causes of populism. While I fully recognize the anti-establishment tenor of populism, it does not follow from this that being opposed to the political class, as it is currently composed in liberal democracies such as the UK and US, amounts to being opposed to democratic politics simpliciter. More plausibly, such anti-establishment sentiment can be seen as motivated by a desire to see a more representative socio-economic cross-section of 'the people' within the political class. That is, in line with the argument offered in the previous chapter, populism can be interpreted as a desire to radicalize rather than liquidate democratic political culture.

The second basic factor motivating the connection between populism and working-class struggle has to do with what Sennett and Cobb (1972) refer to as 'the hidden injuries of class'. This theme will be elaborated on at length in the next chapter, but it is useful to anticipate it at this point. The basic argument is as follows: if modern democracy is crucially motivated by opposition to exploitative economic dependency, any genuine advance in freedom must involve social-economic mechanisms for realizing the transition out of this generalized dependency. The actual mechanism that historically arises to meet this demand for freedom is that of meritocratic advancement. Perceived merit, however, is culturally encoded in such a way that markers of esteem in working-class culture are systematically denigrated. It follows from this that, in the process of gaining relative autonomy, any member of the working class will be obliged to negate their class identity as the price of advancement. This creates, as Sennett and Cobb (1972) identify, a working-class political sentiment of resentment.

As long as the working class enjoys a degree of economic advancement relative to those in other, higher socio-economic classes, the resentment generated by what we might called cultural denigration can be palliated. However, as Thomas Piketty's (2013) *Capital in the Twenty-First Century* argued compellingly, the dynamics of economic equalization in the previous century were a historical anomaly. As Paul Mason (2014) noted in the *Guardian*: 'For Piketty, the long, mid-20th century period of rising equality was a blip, produced by the exigencies of war, the power of organised labour, the need for high taxation, and by demographics and technical innovation.' While anti-establishment sentiment in the US and UK may have peaked after the financial crisis of 2008, arguably it had been gathering steam in the prolonged period of neoliberalization since the early 1980s. It was only when there were gains in neither economic nor cultural capital for the working class that levels of resentment could lead to support for such things as Britain's withdrawal from the European Union and the election of a professedly anti-establishment president such as Donald Trump.

The question focused on in this and forthcoming chapters is the following: If populism stems from justified working-class resentment in the face of neoliberal deprivation and denigration, what would a positive programme of working-class democratic politics look like under current historic conditions? In other words, what does such populism want? In order to be in a position to tackle this question adequately, it is necessary to clarify, in advance, some of the historical connections between working-class struggle and the establishment of modern democratic political culture.

It is also important to acknowledge the simple fact that no historical necessity brought about the political reforms that led to general enfranchisement in places like Britain in the course of the nineteenth century. Victorian liberal theorists and social commentators such as J. S. Mill (1989) and Matthew Arnold (2010), while recognizing the legitimacy and expediency of a gradual process of broadened political enfranchisement, were unambiguous in their insistence on antecedent educational cultivation and moral improvement of the working class. Ardent political and social reformers among the working class did not, however, wait for these conditions to be met, but rather demanded democratization through intellectual argument, social agitation and public demonstration.

It is part of the neoliberal remaking of political and social reality that the historical causes of democratic political culture have become obscured or hidden from view entirely. This forgetting of the origins of modern democracy wreaks havoc with our political discourse on contemporary populism and helps bring about the general consensus that it is, *in toto*, an anti-democratic phenomenon. As set out in Chapter 1, this obfuscation takes the theoretical form of a misconstrual of democracy such that it is seen as the product of ongoing rational consensus. Against this, it was argued in the previous chapter that modern democracy is more adequately seen as an open-ended dynamic dissensus concerning the legitimacy of those who demonstrably hold power within the political community.

Even those interpretations, such as the one offered by Mudde and Kaltwasser (2012), which allow contemporary populism to be either reactionary or progressive in character, fail to grasp the fundamental fact that democratic political culture is grounded in a dynamic of radical dissent. The easiest way of expressing what is being opposed here is to say that democracy is not a classically liberal project, that is, is not a matter of linear social progress and 'good sense' predicated on the 'force of the better argument', in Habermas's (1990) terms.

In asserting an intrinsic connection between democratic political culture and the working-class struggle for material emancipation I am acutely aware of running the risk of presenting what may appear as an inadequate, one-dimensional analysis of contemporary populism. As we have seen, many current interpretations of populism view it through the lens of a disenchanted 'white working class'. As Eatwell and Goodwin note: 'In the shadow of Trump, Brexit and the rise of national populism in Europe, countless writers drew a straight line to an alienated white underclass in America's industrial heartlands, angry pensioners in England's fading seaside resorts and the unemployed in Europe's wastelands' (2018: 17). These authors mount a convincing case that any straightforward argument that populism can be explained through recourse to an ethno-racially homogeneous post-industrial working class does not stand up to scrutiny in light of actual voting patterns.

This does not, however, settle the key question: how is contemporary populism related to democratic political culture? Does it stand in direct opposition to such culture and express a desire for an authoritarian post-democratic condition? Or does populism rather, as argued in the previous chapter, express a desire to renew democracy? Having laid out the argument for this latter interpretation in broad conceptual terms, in this chapter I set out to add a historical dimension to the claim that populism is fundamentally motivated by a desire to renew democratic political culture. This will be done by recapitulating and repurposing E. P. Thompson's account of the rise of the English working class in the late eighteenth and early nineteenth centuries.

What made the English working class?

In his wide-ranging and influential social history, *The Making of the English Working Class*, E. P. Thompson (1968) analyses in great detail the ideological, economic and cultural determinants of the rise of the English working class. For Thompson, there are two principal factors that made the English working class: class consciousness and political-economic organization. A late chapter of Thompson's text, devoted to an analysis of class consciousness, accentuates the role played by the dissemination of radical literature in the form of periodic pamphlets and newsletters. The distribution and discussion of such literature was an aspect of a broader working-class auto-didacticism which fairly rapidly granted to the English working class a historical self-image and sense of political purpose:

> Thus working men formed a picture of the organization of society, out of their own experience and with the help of their hard-won and erratic education, which was above all a political picture ... From 1830 onwards a more clearly defined class consciousness, in the customary Marxist sense, was maturing, in which working people were aware of continuing both old and new battles on their own. (1968: 782)

Recalling Laclau's analysis of progressive populism and the indeterminacy regarding 'the people', it is important to note how Thompson accentuates the existence of significant heterogeneity within the formation of the working class. One can scarcely come away from Thompson's analysis and not be impressed by the sheer complexity of the English working class as he reconstructs its social history. In theoretical terms, the identity of the working class achieved through class consciousness is not a matter of some unchanging self-identical subject; it is rather a question of a relatively unified sense of historical purpose predicated on a constantly changing set of complex social-material conditions. This point is important to underscore, as it allows for working-class politics to be understood in line with a mode of populism precisely not founded on any sense of monolithic identity.

Thompson makes the point of the diversity of the burgeoning English working class in his account of the consumption of radical literature in the early decades of the nineteenth century:

> [I]t is a mistake to see it as a single, undifferentiated 'reading public'. We may say that there were several different 'publics' impinging upon and overlapping each other, but nevertheless organized according to different principles. Among the more important were the commercial public, pure and simple, which might be exploited at times of Radical excitement ... the passive public which the improving societies sought to get at and redeem; and the active, Radical public, which organized itself in the face of the Six Acts and the taxes on knowledge. (1968: 790)

By 'taxes on knowledge' Thompson means the stamp tax imposed on the circulation of Radical literature in the third decade of the nineteenth century. This was a pointedly political move aimed at rendering unaffordable the weekly political pamphlets that had been doing so much to form a nascent English working-class consciousness. Attempting to make such literature and the political education it provided unaffordable was one means to stifle the formation of class consciousness. Another was state censorship in the form of official or 'stamped' literature. Those who produced and distributed 'unstamped' reading material were subject to severe sentences, often many years of imprisonment: 'Perhaps 500 people were prosecuted for the production and sale of the "unstamped". From 1816 (indeed, from 1792) until 1836 the contest involved, not only the editors, booksellers, and printers, but also many hundreds of newsvendors, hawkers, and voluntary agents' (Thompson, 1968: 801).

For Thompson, self-education was another key factor in the rise of working-class consciousness. Given limited literacy among the working class in the nineteenth century, auto-didacticism in this context did not only or predominantly take the form of solitary study. The various weekly pamphlets and Radical books were often read and discussed in social contexts involving regular face-to-face discussion. As this required some degree of freedom from work, Thompson draws attention to the key role played by the multifarious artisan class that enjoyed a greater degree of self-organization relative to early factory workers.

The artisans were also apt to harbour sentiments of political self-determination on account of their self-image as skilled workers animated by a certain spirit of entrepreneurialism (we will return to this point when discussing work and craft in Chapter 4). Taking things into their own hands was, quite literally, what the artisans did for a living. Translating this into political self-determination was, in this sense, a more plausible step in their social evolution. But this also required concrete social organization predicated on a much broader sense of class interest. It was this broadening of self-interest and political self-image that the educational impact of Radical literature was able to achieve. The transition involved here is one from individual to group autonomy:

> [T]he artisans aspired to an 'independence'. This aspiration colours much of the history of the early working-class Radicalism ... This helps to explain the sudden surge of support towards Owenism at the end of the 1820s – trade union traditions and the yearning for independence were twisted together in the idea of social control over their own means of livelihood; a *collective* independence. (1968: 290)

While the decades following the end of the Napoleonic Wars witnessed rapid increase in economic productivity brought about by technological innovation, a formative factor for the making of the English working class was the sense, experienced acutely by the skilled artisan class, that this economic development did not, on the whole, represent real advance for the working class. As Thompson sums up: 'What we can say with confidence is that the artisan *felt* that his status and standard-of-living were under threat or were deteriorating between 1815 and 1840' (p. 289).

This sense of deterioration in the face of officially promulgated improvement was drawn from consciousness of 'the *general* insecurity of all skills during this period. The very notion of regularity of employment – at one place of work over a number of years for regular hours and at a standard wage – is anachronistic' (p. 274). This insecurity is, in turn, predicated on a more general feature of the period in question: 'The first half of the nineteenth century must be seen as a period of chronic under-employment, in which the skilled trades are like islands threatened on every side by technological innovation and by the inrush of unskilled or juvenile labour' (p. 269).

This picture of the historical conditions of workers bears comparison with the period of mature neoliberalism, particularly following the Great Recession that began in 2008, which produced across wealthy liberal democracies acute economic and social precariousness (see Piketty, 2013). The same divergence between significant increases in general wealth production and lower standards of living for the vast majority in society is clearly on display. The ideologues of free trade in the nineteenth century essentially peddled the same political ideology as today's mainstream politicians: what is good for the economy must be good for all workers.

If we wish to draw more radical and constructive conclusions from the current wave of populism, then we need to move beyond the prevalent reactive alarmism. Contemporary populism, as I argue throughout this book, is not primarily the product of the last few years of party politics. Its roots lie in the long neoliberal socio-economic transformation that dates back to the 1970s. However, seeing current populism as a countermovement to neoliberal governance is, in itself, of comparatively little worth if we cannot conceive and formulate a positive mode of democratic politics that would credibly take the place of the current neoliberal dispensation. Hence, delineating what organized political opposition to the neoliberal paradigm could amount to, on the theoretical plane, is a central task of the current analysis.

Any materialist account of political history has to be grounded in an understanding of the past. No real progress can be made understanding the intrinsic connections between democracy and populism without attempting to reconstruct, in broad terms, the historical conditions under which the modern democratic political community emerged. This does not imply that any progressive formulation of liberal democracy in the future would amount to a return to the past. It is, rather, a question of recapturing a coherent image of democracy grounded in the realities of its emergence and development in the past. Only in light of such a vivid image of democracy can the progressive potentialities of contemporary populism be grasped.

The social conditions of the early nineteenth century are hardly comparable, in any precise empirical sense, to those in play two centuries later. There are, nevertheless, pertinent parallels, principally with respect to working-class self-organization and acts of ideological and material emancipation that must be reformulated if the social pathologies of the neoliberal order are to be undermined and eventually done away with. In order to think beyond the neoliberal conjuncture, we need social and labour history to reinvigorate our collective political imagination. In the current moment, we are faced with the task of highlighting the intrinsic connections between working-class consciousness and democratic culture in order to draw out the important lessons of contemporary populism. Doing this will allow us to think, and eventually act, beyond the sclerotic condition of contemporary liberal democratic party politics.

Working-class political praxis

The burgeoning self-education of the English working class, documented in fine-grained detail in Thompson's (1968) social history, was by no means simply a matter of intellectual curiosity and self-improvement. In the face of the neoliberal consolidation of formal education and communications media in our own times, it becomes increasingly difficult to appreciate how the effort to educate and inform oneself can have a genuine capacity for collective social change and political transformation. David Harvey relates how, in the wake of another period of explosive social change in the 1960s, institutions of higher education were targeted by neoliberal advocates as a crucial test case of ideological capture: 'Charting the spread of ideas is always difficult, but by 1990 or so most economics departments in the major research universities as well as the business schools were dominated by neoliberal modes of thought. The importance of this should not be underestimated' (2005: 54).

More generally, it is worthwhile noting the historical irony of the role of formal education in the current context of neoliberalization. While more people than ever across wealthy liberal democracies avail themselves of some kind of tertiary education, the impact that this has on collective work conditions and economic security is highly questionable. As far as higher education for England and Wales is concerned, I have personally lived through a twenty-year transition in which a university education for the working class in the UK has gone from something freely available (with the required exam results) and supported by modest state-funded maintenance grants, to a consumer choice costing over £9,000 per academic year.

This reality is a direct result of neoliberalization, which transforms all collective goods into matters of individual entrepreneurial risk-taking. Neoliberal education is a matter of investing in one's own future and – so political good sense dictates – should not be paid for by general taxation. But this just captures the conditions that govern entry to post-secondary education. The exit conditions are, arguably, the truer test. While it remains the case that students from working-class backgrounds do improve their chances of work and material improvement by receiving this education, the economic conditions encountered by today's graduates are extremely bleak. In addition, there are the issues of working-class identity, which tend to exclude graduates from reaping the kinds of benefits university offers others of a higher-class status. As Jin and Ball (2019: 13) note: 'Class profoundly shapes the way students experience university and other fields of education. Educational experiences, for working-class students, are rarely liberating and transformative, the working-class habitus always haunts them and constrains them and consumes their new experiences, and the possibilities that arise of a different future.'

Even where well-paid employment is found, job security and union protections at work are increasingly scarce. While in the UK there has been much recent discussion of the so-called gig economy, little has been done to curb the current excesses of worker exploitation through policy and legislation. Relentless neoliberal restructuring of the labour market has brought about the rise of ubiquitous precarious employment, especially for younger workers. This has had a significant impact on the traditional role of trades unions in leveraging the power of collective bargaining relative to business owners and administrators. Gumbrell-McCormick (2011: 298) observes, in a study of ten European countries, that trade union membership 'is generally lower than that of workers in "traditional" stable and full-time forms of work. In the UK, for example, 28 per cent of permanent workers are in trade unions as opposed to only 16 per cent of temporary workers. Similarly, 30 per cent of full-time workers are union members, but only 22 per cent of part-time.'

In light of the current predicament of formal education, it is enlightening to consider further Thompson's account of the role self-education played in the formation of the English working class. Such reflection helps us to compare current conditions, where post-secondary adult education has become a key entrepreneurial sector in the post-industrial neoliberal market, with efforts at self-education by English workers in the early nineteenth century. Such a comparison readily reveals the hollowness of claims that current university education is anything like an effective means of overcoming structural inequalities engineered by neoliberal economics.

As the cases Thompson (1968) relates vividly depict, the very fact that the state made it so difficult for the working class to educate itself gave rise to manifold insurrectionary practices. Here it is a matter not just of what was read, discussed and learnt, but also of how this was happening. As Thompson accentuates, these fights over freedom of thought and speech were not cast in the customary bourgeois mode of individual intellectual enlightenment. Rather, they went hand in hand with collective political agitation, representing a veritable cascade of political praxis that advanced the cause of working-class political self-representation:

> It is as if the English nation entered a crucible in the 1790s and emerged after the Wars in a different form. Between 1811 and 1813, the Luddite crisis; in 1817 the Pentridge Rising; in 1819, Peterloo; throughout the next decade the proliferation of trade union activity, Owenite propaganda, Radical journalism, the Ten Hours Movement, the revolutionary crisis of 1831–2; and, beyond that, the multitude of movements which made up Chartism. (1968: 209)

The 'revolutionary crisis' Thompson refers to here centres on the build-up to the Reform Bill of 1832. This was preceded by eighteen months of intense working-class agitation which had the political establishment increasingly concerned. The key factor that forestalled the kind of truly revolutionary activity that would occur across Europe in 1848, and later during the period of the Paris Commune of 1871, was, in Thompson's view, the successful separation of middle-class from working-class Radicalism. This amounted to a compromise that 'might not weaken, but strengthen both the State and property-rights against the working-class threat' (p. 899).

While the 1832 Reform Bill brought about a modest extension of the male franchise, it fell far short of the demands of the working-class Radicals. Thompson cites the example of Leeds, which, out of a total population of 124,000, saw an additional 355 workmen granted the vote, the majority of whom earned well above the working-class average wage for the time. While the working-class Radical press heaped scorn on this derisory extension of the franchise, on the level of praxis the working class organized themselves through 'the great union wave of 1832–4' (p. 282). This movement was the culmination of a generations-long effort to protect certain sectors of skilled labour from the ever-present threat of being undercut by cheaper, 'dishonourable' workers. While protecting pay was the chief concern, this came in conjunction with a further demand for limited hours of work:

> The second critical period is 1833–5, when on the crest of the great trade union wave attempts were made to 'equalize' conditions, shorten working hours in the honourable trade and suppress dishonourable work ... The economic historian should see the cases of the Tolpuddle Martyrs and the great lock-outs of 1834 as being as consequential for all grades of labour as the radicals and trade unionists of the time held them to be. (pp. 284–5)

The year 1834 saw the introduction of a new Poor Law which, in formal legal terms, ended the tradition of 'outdoor' relief and obliged those seeking economic means to combat dire poverty to do so from within the workhouse. As Thompson documents, this legislative change was predicated on an ideological admixture of Methodist work ethic and utilitarian social thinking that saw poverty as a consequence of indolence that called for character reform. The workhouse provided a disciplinary space where the poor could be reformed through both negative social stigma and positive reinforcement. For Thompson, this new management of the working poor was a direct manifestation of ruling-class oppression exerted on an insurrectionary working class:

> The Act of 1834, and its subsequent administration by men like Chadwick and Kay, was perhaps the most sustained attempt to impose an ideological dogma, in defiance of human need, in English history. No discussion of the standard-of-living in 1834 can make sense which does not examine the consequences, as troubled Boards of Guardians tried to apply Chadwick's insane Instructional Circulars as to the abolition or savage restriction of out-relief in depressed industrial centres. (p. 295)

Despite the extreme systemic deprivation and humiliation experienced, within a decade of the passing of the 1834 Poor Law the total population of Union workhouses across England and Wales numbered around 200,000. 'The most eloquent testimony to the depths of poverty,' Thompson observes, 'is in the fact that they were tenanted at all' (p. 296).

The point of drawing attention to such legislative and institutional history is to give a sense of how class consciousness and praxis are unavoidably oppositional. As recounted, the working class was formed through a sequence of common acts of resistance that granted a sense of common interest and purpose. This common sensibility or culture – 'class consciousness' – was not miraculously fabricated from within a working class already, somehow, aware of itself as such. It was a product of concrete, drawn-out historical political-economic struggles, where organized action met with certain responses by the ruling classes, using the levers of government to frame a punitive legal context of oppression. Social class, as Thompson highlights in the preface to his study, is not an abstract social category or essential feature of some sort of abstracted social formation or structure. Instead, it is 'something which in fact happens (and can be shown to have happened) in human relationships' (p. 9). If class is a product of shared experiences giving rise to a sense of identity of interests opposed to the interests of others, then 'class-consciousness is the way in which these experiences are handled in cultural terms: embodied in traditions, value-systems, ideas, and institutional forms' (p. 10).

The oppositional origin and nature of class consciousness can also be illustrated by highlighting the sense of injustice and inequality lived through by workers over the course of early industrialization in England. The following passage makes evident the parallels between Thompson's account and the contemporary sensibility of populism:

> In fifty years of the Industrial Revolution the working-class share of the national product had almost certainly fallen relative to the share of the property-owning and professional classes. The 'average' working man remained very close to subsistence level at a time when he was surrounded by the evidence of the increase of national wealth, much of it transparently the object of his own labour, and passing, by equally transparent means, into the hands of his employers. In psychological terms, this felt very much like a decline in standards. His own share in the 'benefits of economic progress' consisted of more potatoes, a few articles of cotton clothing for his family, soap and candles, some tea and sugar. (p. 351)

It is not hard, in our own times, to find politicians preaching what is essentially the same doctrine of generalized economic progress meted out to the working class two hundred years ago. An analogous sense of seeing improvement for others amid worsening conditions for most workers is also manifestly widespread. But it clearly makes all the difference to be living through an epoch when the working class is, for the first time, coming to consciousness of itself as a political force, as opposed to our own moment in time when the mere mention of working-class politics sounds like an embarrassing anachronism. Hence, the various rebranding efforts for oppositional politics.

Reformulating working-class politics in the twenty-first century is, admittedly, a daunting task not reducible to glib appeals to what Srnicek and Williams (2016) refer to as 'folk politics'. They define folk politics as 'a set of strategic assumptions that threaten to debilitate the left, rendering it unable to scale up, create lasting change or expand beyond particular interests' (2016: 9–10). One of the key features embedded in leftist folk politics, Srnicek and Williams assert, is a pronounced tendency towards 'prefigurative politics': a kind of performative anticipation of direct democracy, where the desired progressive future is acted out in microcosm. The most powerful and salient illustrative case of this tendency is the Occupy movement of 2011. The essential problem with such prefigurative politics, according to Srnicek and Williams, is the inability to match political praxis to the scale of the dominant political paradigm: 'The reality of complex, globalised capitalism is that small interventions consisting of relatively non-scalable actions are highly unlikely to ever be able to reorganise our socioeconomic system' (2016: 29).

These warnings against the current formulation of progressive politics have to be taken seriously. In part, the failings of prefigurative politics account for the appearance and success of current populism. If a large tranche of the working class feels that its interests are not being furthered either by government or by what is recognized as the advanced position of leftist political praxis, then it is hardly surprising that populist sentiment takes root. While the universalism of the Marxist appeal to 'workers of the world' can be readily deconstructed by those who appeal to the affective bonds and causes of local communities or identity politics, it is a mistake to reject the whole legacy of working-class solidarity in favour of smaller-scale struggles of identity-based politics. Only when the history of working-class struggle is grasped as a dynamic and fragile construction of collective practice maintained over generations and manifested in myriad forms of institutionalized solidarity, can its relevance to the future of democratic politics be adequately recognized.

Where were the English working class?

It may sound odd to pose this question concerning the whereabouts of the English working class. The pertinence of the question stems from the generalized assumption that working-class culture arose predominantly or even exclusively in the industrialized cities of England. Thompson's social history, in addition to Raymond Williams's (1973) complementary assessment of the rise of working-class consciousness in the context of English literature of the time, makes clear that social change in the rural context is an element not to be overlooked. Williams's (1973) *The Country and the City*, as the title suggests, considers social and political history through the lens of urban–rural connections. In many ways, Thompson had already set the stage for this.

A key issue, dealt with by both authors in some detail, is that of the enclosure of the commons. The numerous parliamentary acts of enclosure entailed the removal of informal, customary rights held by local residents of rural settlements in England and the UK more generally: rights to small-scale cultivation, grazing, harvesting and foraging in open fields and woodland. In referencing 'the commons', therefore, it is important to recognize that we are speaking about usage as opposed to ownership rights. The rationale for enclosure was intensifying agricultural production in line with new farming methods and machinery. According to the official UK Parliament website: 'From the 1750s enclosure by parliamentary Act became the norm. Overall, between 1604 and 1914 over 5,200 enclosure Bills were enacted by Parliament which related to just over a fifth of the total area of England, amounting to some 6.8 million acres' (UK Parliament, n.d.).

The economic, social and cultural impact of the numerous acts of enclosure, especially between 1750 and 1850, is a matter of continued academic contestation (see Mingay, 1997). Due in no small way to left-leaning social historians such as Thompson, the enclosures have become an iconic instance of what Marx called 'primitive accumulation' in the context of British history and the understanding of the politics of capitalist industrialization more generally. In the face of contemporary neoliberal governance and the fact that the majority of the world's population now live in urban centres, in the twenty-first century Marxist critical geographers and social theorists have appealed to a contemporary need to establish a new urban commons. This has been proposed in terms of a generalized 'right to the city' that empowers urban residents to counter draconian policing methods, surveillance technologies and the privatization of public spaces (see Mitchell, 2003; Brenner, 2011; Harvey, 2012; Merrifield, 2014).

Thompson's verdict on the acts of enclosure that became prevalent across the English countryside from the last third of the eighteenth century is that they represented 'a plain enough case of class robbery, played according to fair rules of property and law laid down by a parliament of property-owners and lawyers' (1968: 237–8). He elaborates: 'But what was "perfectly proper" in terms of capitalist property-relations involved, none the less, a rupture of the traditional integument of village custom and of right: and the social violence of enclosure consisted precisely in the drastic, total imposition upon the village of capitalist property definitions' (p. 238).

The kind of class oppression meted out to the rural workers of England in the name of economic productivity entailed denying them their customary access to land use. This had the immediate effect of rendering field labourers dependent on wage-earning to supply their basic needs. Where such sources of income were precarious or non-existent, direct provision became necessary. This gave rise in 1795 to the Speenhamland system of 'outdoor relief' (supplements to income or capping of prices on basic goods) which, during the Napoleonic Wars, sought to shelter rural workers from inflated grain prices. According to Thompson, the perpetuation of this system 'was ensured by the demand of the larger farmers – in an industry which has exceptional requirements for occasional or casual labour – for a permanent cheap labour reserve' (p. 244).

Williams (1973) underscores this connection between the Speenhamland system and the rapid transition to farmland consolidation. In essence, he sees this effort to subsidize the agricultural labourer's income as a typically muddle-headed attempt of bourgeois social amelioration of economic forces which would, in time, only exacerbate the very condition the laws were meant to improve. What Thompson calls, with reference to the Enclosure Acts, the 'total imposition upon the village of capitalist property definitions' (1968: 238), Williams sees, in allied terms, as a relentless process of primitive accumulation on the part of a ruling class appropriating ever larger parcels of land: 'In all previous settlements [the agricultural labourer] had been bearing the real cost of expansion and improvement; but now he bore it, with increasing emphasis, as a pauper, an object of charity: a fate that was foreshadowed in this place and that, this period and that, through many earlier generations, but that now, in the widening crisis, grew to something like a system' (Williams, 1973: 183).

The political economy of late eighteenth- and early nineteenth-century agriculture indicates that, in many ways, the English working class was made in the countryside. The generally held belief about industrialization then and now is that it essentially involved mass migration from the country to the city. In the case of English history during the Industrial Revolution, as Williams points out, this can only be asserted with significant qualification:

> From the 1850s to the 1890s, emigration from the villages to the towns, especially in certain parts of the country, became heavy. This was not, in the strict sense, a rural depopulation, though a few counties suffered permanent absolute losses. More generally what happened was that the rural population failed to grow, while the urban population continued to grow dramatically, in a general population increase, and while emigration to other lands notably increased. (1973: 188)

Earlier in the century, Speenhamland had been replaced by the Poor Law of 1834 which, formally at least, outlawed 'outdoor relief' and established a system of workhouses ('indoor relief'). In Thompson's stark judgement, the new Poor Law 'had a single tendency: to destroy the last vestige of control by the labourer over his own wage and working life' (1968: 248). This tendency had already become apparent to rural labourers through the process of enclosure: 'To the argument of greed a new argument was added for general enclosure – that of social discipline ... Ideology was added to self-interest. It became a matter of public-spirited policy for the gentleman to remove cottagers from the commons, reduce his labourers to dependence, pare away at supplementary earnings, drive out the smallholder' (pp. 242–3).

What is vital to note about these features of the history of agricultural political economy is that they provided a provisional but profound experience of class-based systemic oppression. While the mass agitation that would break out with the Chartist movement in the 1830s was predominantly an urban phenomenon, it can be argued that the crucial gestational period of English working-class culture occurred among rural labourers between the 1790s and 1830s. The historically crucial experience of these workers basically boiled down to severe erosion of social-economic independence due to loss of access to land. This is a matter of diminished material autonomy, namely precisely the condition which the 'precariat' of advanced neoliberal governance currently finds itself in. This makes plausible a more or less constant working-class experience of economic dependence and devaluation under capitalist economic production and social reproduction.

Rather than thinking of agricultural labourers on the notorious terms of 'rural idiocy' (i.e. apolitical isolation) proclaimed by Marx and Engels (2004) in *The Communist Manifesto* of 1848, Thompson and Williams invite us to view them as the forebears of a later full-blown working-class culture. As Thompson notes: 'It is an historical irony that it was not the rural labourers but the urban workers who mounted the greatest coherent national agitation for the return of the land. Some of them were sons and grandsons of labourers, their wits sharpened by the political life of the towns, freed from the shadows of the squire. Some – supporters of the [Chartist] Land Plan – were weavers and artisans of rural descent' (1968: 255–6). In other words, while the truly self-conscious working class can be said to be an urban phenomenon of the 1830s, the crucible in which working-class consciousness was forged was the struggle over access to usable land fought across the English countryside by the preceding generations of rural labourers.

In this connection, Williams often alludes to his own experience of growing up in a small rural village in the border country of south Wales in the 1920s and 1930s. His idea of culture as a 'structure of feeling' is very much animated by this experience of rural village life, with its intricate and intense networks of informal reciprocal obligations. By contrast, coexistence in the city is typically characterized by a sense of largely benign indifference to one's neighbours. In some of his later writings Williams drew attention to the capacity for small-scale communities to unite in some form of political praxis as 'militant particularism'. In an essay from 1981, for example, Williams makes the following remark:

> The unique and extraordinary character of working-class self-organization has been that it has tried to connect particular struggles to a general struggle in one quite special way. It has set out, as a movement, to make real what is at first sight the extraordinary claim that the defence and advancement of certain particular interests, properly brought together, are in fact in the general interest. That, after all, is the moment of transition to an idea of socialism. (1989: 249)

Williams's words here echo Thompson's prefatory remarks about class, where he cautions against turning the notions of class and class consciousness into things abstracted from the concrete experience of particular people in a particular time and place: 'By class I understand a historical phenomenon, unifying a number of disparate and seemingly unconnected events, both in the raw material of experience and in consciousness. I emphasize that it is a *historical* phenomenon. I do not see class as a "structure", nor even as a "category", but as something which in fact happens (and can be shown to have happened) in human relationships' (Thompson, 1968: 9).

We must keep this account in mind when attempting to understand populism as a function of working-class politics. If we make this attempt, then populism ceases to be grasped, predominantly or exclusively, as a matter of charismatic demagogues and the canny manipulation of a gullible, xenophobic populace. Instead, we learn to see it as a complex expression of underlying class dynamics. The social history of working-class struggle, as portrayed by Thompson and Williams, is characterized by a deep underlying ambivalence towards parliamentary politics. In one sense, it is possible to view the creation of the British Labour Party as a clear translation of working-class interest into party political organization. But radical social historians stress the constant tension involved in this equation. Militancy, in all its guises, was not transcended once workers had a party to represent their class interests.

If we follow Thompson's understanding of class, what underlies it is a living stream of intergenerational experience that retains a consistent 'structure of feeling' despite all variations of place and time. As such, there will always be pronounced tensions between the dynamic lived experience of the working class and any party historically founded to represent that class's interests. With this in mind, my contention is that contemporary populism should be grasped as an appeal to recast, in radical ways, the manner in which working-class interests are advanced through the party structures of representative liberal democracy. Exploring the social history of the emergence of modern democracy serves to remind us that working-class struggle antedated the arrival of any party to represent its interests. If now, in an age of populism, established bonds between party and people appear broken, then we should see this as a sign that working-class interests require a new, historically unprecedented formulation of democratic politics.

Chartism: the working class comes of age

In the previous section, it was shown how the seminal struggles of the English working class centred on access to land within a rural population increasingly confronted with the manifold pressures exerted by agrarian capitalism. This leads us to conclude, somewhat surprisingly, that the English working class come into existence in the country rather than the city. This should not be understood as downplaying the crucial significance of the historically unparalleled migration of the population from the country to the city. It is rather a question of the lived experience that those migrating workers brought to their new urban surroundings. As Thompson puts it, 'rural memories were fed into the urban working-class through innumerable personal experiences' (1968: 253–4).

None of this entails the denial that working-class politics was subject to significant change and intensification in the face of rapid urbanization. Along with this urbanization, technological innovations in transportation (the railways) and communications (the telegraph) had immediate widespread social impact from the 1830s on. Relatively isolated rural communities were giving way to a context of the urban 'masses'. In terms of working-class politics, the central challenge was, following Williams's notion of militant particularism, to make good on 'the extraordinary claim that the defence and advancement of certain particular interests, properly brought together, are in fact in the general interest' (Williams, 1989: 249).

It is in this context, following working-class disappointment at the property qualifications attached to the 1832 Reform Act which widened the male franchise, that the short-lived but unprecedentedly widespread political movement of Chartism arose. In a seminal and meticulous study of the Chartist movement, E. P. Thompson's wife and fellow social historian, Dorothy Thompson, notes: 'The great Reform Act of 1832 had defined more clearly than at any time before or since in British history, and more clearly than had been done in any other country, a qualification for the inclusion in the political institutions of the country based entirely on the possession of property and the possession of a regular income ... A movement to extend the franchise was bound to divide the country on class lines' (1984: 5).

Chartism, described by Dorothy Thompson (1984) as 'the world's first labour movement', was announced with the publication of the People's Charter in 1838. While the 'Six Points' of the Charter – including, crucially, the call to remove all property qualifications on the franchise for men over the age of twenty-one – had all been advanced in the previous century, the historical novelty of Chartism as a political movement consisted in the fact that 'it was national: it took the same form in all parts of the country. It was also to be backed by simultaneous meetings of support throughout the country and by a National Convention – or anti-parliament – to supervise its organization, collection and presentation' (Thompson, 2015: 153). A decade after the publication of the Charter, in the revolutionary year of 1848, the Chartists held firm to their ruling idea that working-class interests would be best served by reform rather than revolution: 'the road to reform was seen to lie through the enlargement of the political system to include the working class, not through the overthrow of the system as such' (Thompson, 2015: 154).

One of the key matters of debate within Chartist circles related to the prospects of 'moral force' as opposed to 'physical force'. Certainly, in the early years of the Chartist movement (1838–39) there were localized uprisings involving law-breaking. But, for the most part, the path of moral force to achieve parliamentary reform was pursued. This dichotomy remains a key feature of contemporary political activism or 'direct action', where the division is generally seen to turn on the espousal or refusal of violence (Wood, 2014). The notion of political violence calls for careful analysis, though I shall not pursue this issue here. The key point about Chartism in the current context is how it marked a certain maturation point in the emergence of working-class consciousness. As Dorothy Thompson makes clear, it was a matter of realizing a unified, nationwide political platform, which could exert concerted pressure on the political establishment through the advance of specific demands.

It is important to note too that Chartism also embodied a certain ambivalence concerning the way the working class should relate to the system of parliamentary democracy. In the first half of the nineteenth century, expansions of general suffrage by no means brought with them advances in working-class interests. Both before and after the rise of Chartism, therefore, we see a flowering of many instances of working-class self-organization – trade unions, mutual societies, cooperatives, and so forth – that attempt to realize such interests above and beyond any efforts directed towards national politics and extending the franchise. Thus, while Chartism represents the point at which the English working class comes of age, the movement's ambivalence towards the bureaucratic political system and the sufficiency of universal suffrage is a key feature.

A parallel ambivalence clearly inhabits contemporary populism, whether in the form of the Brexit sentiment that desires to bring governance closer to the people (and away from Brussels) or in the 'America first' appeal of Trump. There seem to be two threads of political desire tightly woven together here: on the one hand, a wish to reinvigorate national politics in the name of 'the people'; on the other hand, an anti-establishment animus that sees governmental bureaucracy as opposed to the true interests of citizens. Equally, it is difficult to say whether these two objects of desire neatly fall into the reform versus revolution dichotomy. My point, in this context, is that the historical advance of working-class politics contains within itself a certain ambivalence about empowerment through political representation. While widening the franchise was clearly a key goal of Radical politics in nineteenth-century England, the ultimate claims of the movement called for much more diffused and multifarious means of material autonomy.

In terms of a maturing working-class consciousness, Chartism is involved in a further tension: that between 'utopian' and 'scientific' socialism as identified by Engels (2003) in his late essay from 1880. The earlier utopian phase, considered in its British context, is typified by the followers of the progressive industrialist Robert Owen who conceived of social improvement in terms of self-sufficient industrial communities organized in a spirit of mutualism advancing the common good. What E. P. Thompson calls Owenism's 'dream of a cooperative community upon the land' fed into the Chartist political vision in the 1830s and 1840s, thereby giving 'the myth gargantuan dimensions' (1968: 254–5).

Accordingly, Owen's idea that the social and moral shortcomings of industrialization could be made good by the founding of beneficent autarchic communities – an idea echoed by his French contemporary Charles Fourier – found their place in the Chartist vision. In Thompson's words, 'the yearning for land arises again and again, twisted in with the outworker's desire for an "independence", from the days of Spence to the Chartist Land Plan and beyond' (1968: 254). Quoting a speech by the Chartist leader Feargus O'Connor, Thompson is careful to qualify his description of this yearning for control of the land as a 'myth': 'but the myth of the lost paternalist community became a force in its own right – perhaps as powerful a force as the utopian projections of Owen and the Socialists. To say it was a "myth" is not to say it was all false; rather, it is a montage of memories, an "average" in which every loss and every abuse is drawn into one total' (1968: 255).

The retroactive force of collective memory, taken largely from pre-enclosure times, entwines with the political programme of Chartism in a largely nostalgic and historically questionable manner. In other words, the 'myth' of the working-class community free to work its own land in dignity and independence is a political desire of the future drawing on overgeneralized elements of a lived past. As Thompson (1968) carefully states, this does not make it untrue, though it is fair to say that a pathos of nostalgia animates the political passion. Williams, too, questions the idealization of this pre-enclosure working-class idyll:

> What they have is then a relative and fortunate independence, in an interval of settlement which we can be glad lasted many men's lifetimes. But it is not necessarily an order that we can oppose to what succeeded it, when the same neighbouring gentry showed their interest in a different way and enclosed the commons. The rural class-system was already there, and men were living as they could, sometimes well, in its edges, its margins, its as yet ungrasped and undeveloped areas. (Williams, 1973: 101)

This recognition of shared memory is, I believe, a crucial element and driving force in working-class politics. As Williams is especially skilled at drawing out, such a politics tends to flourish in the momentary and marginal interstices of capitalist discipline. If, following Thompson (1968), we recognize working-class politics to be inhabited and led by 'myths' of independence, then this will help to explain why the simplistic and, many would argue, spurious populist appeal to 'Take back control' was so effective. One lesson we can draw from a radical social history of the working class is that the appeal to freedom antedates the currently dominant formulation of neoliberal liberty centred on consumer choice. This allows us, in turn, to see in the current appeal of populism a potential reactivation of another, more profound call to freedom in the form of a generalized condition of material self-determination.

As we have seen, in the case of Chartism such an appeal to enhanced material freedom was articulated as a demand for ownership and usage of the land. Even if it was overlaid with nostalgic and romantic counter-memories of a relatively free, pre-industrial manner of rural life, the Chartist Land Plan was much more than a futile flight of fancy propagated by a dying political movement. As Dorothy Thompson notes, the Plan showed political strength and tactical versatility rather than defeatism: 'As the [1840s] proceeded [Chartists] were turning to self-help of various kinds, trying against the odds of lack of means, alternating overwork and unemployment and the increasing presence of police and military in their communities, to set up their own institutions. The Land Plan provided an organizing focus for all the localities' (1984: 306).

The Plan, which was in existence between 1845 and 1851, offered subscribers the chance to acquire small plots of land (usually a few acres) which they could cultivate and build upon. When the scheme was wound up, after being declared illegal due to its status as a lottery (not all subscribers could be guaranteed allocation of land), some 70,000 Chartist members sought to reclaim invested funds. This gives a sense of the popularity of the Land Plan. One of the generally recognized flaws of the plan was the assumption that subscribers would already possess sufficient working knowledge to farm. Given participation in the Plan by urban workers this was seldom the case. Another, more obviously political criticism of the Plan is that it failed to identify correctly the core problem for the industrialized proletariat, namely that it was not a lack of land ownership, but rather the political economy of private property itself that stood in the way of working-class freedom.

In many ways, however, these criticisms of Chartism fail to grasp the true historical achievement of the movement, namely that it marked the coming of age of working-class consciousness. To assert this in no way precludes recognition that the Chartist moment necessarily entailed a hybrid consciousness containing elements pointing the way to future developments, but also reaching back, no doubt in idealized ways, to earlier struggles over access and usage of rural land. Assuming anything else would oblige us to look at Chartism as the unlikely moment at which a self-conscious British working class appeared on the scene already in a full-blown form. Fundamentally, this means that any credible appeal to the historical formation of working-class politics must recognize the heterogeneity not only of the social identity of those falling within this class, but also of the ideals and demands through which such politics articulates itself. The 'incoherence' of contemporary populism can then be seen in the context of the multifarious and historically unstable dynamic of working-class self-consciousness and political praxis.

Populism and the history of the working class

This chapter has considered aspects of the formation of English working-class culture as described and analysed by the Thompsons and Raymond Williams. These accounts were given by representatives of a generation of British writers who had themselves come from working-class backgrounds and entered the intellectual milieu of formal education via a politically engaged adult education movement. Clearly, they saw themselves, in one way or another, as witnesses to a heritage of working-class self-education and activism stretching back many generations. The principal purpose of this chapter has been to offer a historical-material basis for the underlying thesis of this book, namely that contemporary populism should be seen as a potential renewal of democracy.

What I have tried to establish in this chapter is that working-class consciousness and sense of identity arose in Britain when the manifold experience of localized struggle gave rise to a sense of shared challenges that could be met by advancing specific demands. The history of two such demands (expanded suffrage and access to land) has been briefly sketched. What has been described is, admittedly, only a very limited and inadequate account of the formation of the English working class. But it offers a sufficient thread to follow when attempting to explain the relationship between working-class struggle, democratic culture and populism.

As Eatwell and Goodwin note of the early twentieth-century rise of the British Labour Party: 'It was also driven by a strong sense of class consciousness, a belief that Labour was creating a new and more equitable Britain, which was reinforced by strong working-class group identities in solidaristic mining villages or shipbuilding towns' (2018: 272). But if, as Panitch and Leys observe, the rise and electoral success of New Labour in the 1990s and first decade of the twentieth-first century was recognized as 'repudiating crucial concerns which social democracy had contributed to the struggle for democracy and social justice in the twentieth century' (2001: 287), then it is not hard to see here a traumatic experience of loss for the British working class. This loss can be plausibly seen as entailing a kind of collective political disorientation, as working-class voters are unmoored from 'allegiances ... often "inherited" during childhood' (Eatwell and Goodwin, 2018: 270). This loss of coherent party-political affiliation is crucial, I believe, in understanding the phenomenon of populism in Britain and other liberal democracies.

In the following chapter, we will consider a cluster of social analyses from the late 1950s to the early 1970s that, in various ways, situate the working class at a key turning point in the political history of liberal democracy. It is only when we consider a nuanced and sympathetic account of British working-class culture such as that offered by Richard Hoggart (2009 [1957]) that it becomes possible to recognize how the transition to neoliberal governance in the 1980s all but destroyed it. In simple terms, the transition from the current to the following chapter is a matter of retelling another crucial period in the collective experience of the British working class.

If populism is to be considered a phenomenon intrinsically connected to the role of the working class in contemporary politics, then it is necessary to understand some basic elements of the historical development of this class. The salience of class to the phenomenon of populism more generally is something I will tackle in Chapter 4, when the nature of contemporary work is analysed and critiqued. In the next chapter, my immediate concern is to sketch out, drawing largely from Hoggart's (2009) account, the basic lineaments of working-class life. In such a sketch we will be able to see, in faint outline, the potentiality of the populist phenomenon that now confronts us in all its disturbing vividness and virulence.

3

The invention of working-class culture

The culture of the British working class

The preceding analysis of the rise of the British working class makes clear that many cultural elements were present in its inception: religious, literary and educational. As the nineteenth century wore on, however, a distinct trend arose in reaction to the rise of the British working class. This trend was directed by the basic idea that culture, in its 'proper' sense, was something intrinsically alien to the working class; something into which this class needed to be inducted. In other words, the working class suffered from a distinct deficit of culture. The most eloquent and effective proponent of this perspective was the Victorian essayist and social commentator Matthew Arnold. Arnold became the spokesperson for an enlightened middle class keen to distance itself, on the one hand, from an uneducated working class and, on the other, from a 'barbarian' aristocracy. While Arnold's position, in some senses at least, acknowledged the inevitability of the rise of the British working class, the key thing was to insist on the need to improve it through exposure to 'high' culture. The principal means of such improvement, of course, would be education.

The 1870 Education Act was a key moment in British political history. For the first time, the social need for state-sanctioned universal education was acknowledged and put into action. However, as Williams (1961) relates, there were from the first mixed motives for such educational reform. The key division in debates at the time was between the economic and democratic imperatives: was universal education required so that the British economy could have a sufficient number of skilled workers or in order to ensure a minimum level of competence throughout an expanded electorate? Of course, these two arguments for educational provision could be seen as mutually reinforcing, but placing the emphasis on one or the other made a good deal of difference. The fact that the economic rationale, then as now, prevailed, was decisive for the political role of the British working class. If we educate primarily for the sake of economic expediency rather than for the ends of democratic participation, then we make clear where the priorities of state action lie.

The subordination of popular education to economic imperatives made one thing abundantly clear: the working class could not expect to be indulged in any desire for intrinsic self-development. The injury thereby inflicted upon the British working class has been as profound as it has been lasting. Coming on the heels of the 1867 Reform Act which expanded the franchise, the 1870 Education Act created from the first a highly divisive image of national education. On the one hand, the middle and upper classes could aspire to a 'liberal' education; on the other, the lower classes would be granted an education befitting their economic role. The point here is not that the universal extension of a liberal education would have been the ideal, most progressive, policy to have pursued. Cutting popular education off from the realities of work would have been, in different ways, just as damaging. The point is rather the split in the shared image of education thereby created.

As Williams (1961) makes clear, the whole social history of education in Britain has been profoundly shaped by the exclusivity of a small minority attending the most prestigious institutions of learning and the rest being educated in their shadow. Again, this is crucially important in the context of a putatively democratic culture, as it ingrains a sense of inferiority, incapacity and resentment among the majority. Above all, the modern educational history of Britain has been anything but an exercise in democratic egalitarianism.

Our concern in this chapter is to clarify the relationship between democracy and working-class culture. One extreme, but by no means extinct, position on this is to question the very existence of working-class culture. For Matthew Arnold in 1869, becoming encultured entails being exposed to 'the best that has been thought and said' (Arnold, 2010). According to this view, a culture is essentially all those products of fine art and literature that have been carefully selected, over the generations, by critics distinguished in refinement and taste. In the face of this carefully culled canon, only a Luddite or, in our own times, a confused postmodernist would insist on opening the floodgates to admit the tidal wave of dross and kitsch to be found in the contemporary world. According to this perspective, culture amounts to 'high culture' and is defined in opposition to the vulgar and tasteless. This position is not, however, limited to thinkers who are conservative in outlook. One finds just as virulent a rejection of kitsch and popular art in leftist critical theorists such as Max Horkheimer and Theodor Adorno (1997 [1944]), who champion the stringency of high-modernist experiment against the supposed self-indulgence of everyday entertainment.

It is in the early work of Raymond Williams that we find quite a different outlook on the question of culture. For Williams (1958), the key point is to get beyond the restricted meaning of culture, in terms of an expert selection of the best artefacts. Instead, Williams takes his bearings from the cultural anthropology of the first half of the twentieth century: 'Where *culture* meant a state or habit of mind, or a body of intellectual and moral activities, it means now, also, a whole way of life' (1958: xviii). One of the challenges of this sense of culture is that, as a concrete phenomenon, it is largely implicit and therefore difficult to identify and explicitly analyse. In Williams's celebrated description: 'The term I would suggest to describe it is *structure of feeling*: it is as firm and definite as "structure" suggests, yet it operates in the most delicate and least tangible parts of our activity' (1958: 48). In other words, 'culture' here denotes the warp and woof of everyday experience, lived in its most intimate yet shared manners. This sense of culture grasps it as something very different to the canonized artefacts to be found in museums and galleries or to the items of study in a typical liberal arts programme. Culture has thereby attained such a fluid meaning that we now require additional qualifications to bring it back into focus. Our keyword for doing this in the present context is 'working class'. What, then, is the nature of 'working-class culture'?

Hoggart's analysis of working-class culture

The argument advanced throughout this book is that contemporary populism should be seen as an effort to reassert popular sovereignty as the fundamental principle of democracy. In the British context, such a reassertion is reflected in the Brexit referendum result but is ultimately a consequence of the much longer drawn-out process of neoliberalization beginning in the early 1980s. In the current chapter a further claim is being elaborated and tested, namely that the shift to neoliberal governance should be seen as motivated by a desire to reverse gains made by the working class in the post-Second World War period.

This claim implies that neoliberal governance is intrinsically antagonistic to working-class interests. David Harvey, in *A Brief History of Neoliberalism* (2005), advances just such an argument and offers copious empirical evidence to ground it. Accordingly, Harvey charts the precipitous drop of wealth share among the wealthiest top 1 per cent in the mid-1970s and sees the rise of neoliberalism in the 1980s as primarily a matter of restoring the advantage of this economically dominant class. 'Thirty years of neoliberal freedoms,' he argues, 'have restored power to a narrowly defined capitalist class' (2005: 38). Of course, the class war waged by neoliberalism is generally masked by relentless ideological appeal to market freedoms touted as universally accessible and generally beneficial. But if neoliberalism is a project designed to win back and then radicalize elite economic power, it is just as important to grasp how it also gains strength from a long-standing denigration of working-class values and culture.

It is this connection that leads us back to the thinking of foundational works and figures of British cultural studies from the late 1950s and early 1960s. In the previous chapter, we considered the Thompsons' accounts of the English radical workers' movements of the nineteenth century. These social and political history studies played an important role in defining and defending the efficacy, vibrancy and dignity of English working-class culture. Similarly, the early works of Raymond Williams are engaged in a contemporary struggle to expose the shortcomings and restrictions of the kind of cultural theory rendered commonplace by Victorian essayists such as Matthew Arnold.

One of the dangers to the general recognition of working-class culture perceived by Williams in the 1950s was the growing social influence of the media. This was a period in which the presence of television was beginning to displace the earlier forms of popular entertainment provided by the cinema and radio. The popular press, in particular, was subject to in-depth scrutiny in Williams's early work. This is also a focus of Richard Hoggart's pioneering work, *The Uses of Literacy*, first published in 1957. The question implied by Hoggart's title is: how does the working class stand to change through its access to the products of writing?

Hoggart offers, in the first half of his book, an ethnographic report on the lived experience of the British working class. In the second half, by contrast, he turns to a critique of the popular press and of a creeping commercialism seen to endanger what are presented as key working-class virtues. Hoggart explains in his preface that each half of his book was written as what amounted to a separate project and that he had made little effort to smooth out the unevenness of the material taken as a whole. Hoggart wrote both a sympathetic reconstruction, drawing on many of his own recollected direct experiences of working-class life in a northern English town, and a scholarly critique of the popular press and its impact on contemporary working-class manners and beliefs. While the former draws on the author's early memories and can be readily seen as somewhat nostalgic in tenor, the latter could be viewed as unduly critical of working-class gullibility in the face of modern advertising and media manipulation. Overall, however, Hoggart's analysis still has a refreshingly authentic feel to it and points the way, in its warnings, to developments that largely came to pass over the succeeding decades.

In parallel with Williams's concurrent notion of culture as a 'structure of feeling', Hoggart emphasizes the intimacy and restricted horizons of British working-class culture: 'If we want to capture something of the essence of working-class life in such a phrase, we must say that it is the "dense and concrete life", a life whose main stress is on the intimate, the sensory, the detailed, and the personal' (2009: 87). These attributes of concreteness and density are physically manifested in the typical built environment of British working-class life, with its narrow, cobbled streets and tightly packed terraced housing. In my teenage years, I lived with my mother in such a 'two-up, two-down', with concrete yards placed back to back and separated by a small alleyway. Even in the early 1980s an outside toilet remained intact, despite its obsolescence.

Hoggart makes much of the significance of the family home and how its social life is organized both internally between family members and towards family and friends beyond. This centrality of the family home entails a lack of mobility that appears startling by contemporary standards: 'Unless he gets a council house, a working-class man is likely to live in his local area, perhaps even in the house he "got the keys for" the night before his wedding, all his life. He has little call to move if he is a general labourer, and perhaps hardly more if he is skilled, since his skill is likely to be in a trade for which several nearby works, or some only a tram ride away, provide vacancies' (2009: 48).

While on guard against a tendency to sentimentalize the camaraderie of working-class communities, Hoggart accentuates the lack of ambition that characterizes them. An ingrained suspicion of those who appear to be 'getting above themselves' is a crucial norm, as he sees it, of working-class life: 'Working-class people number several vices among their occupational attitudes, but not those of the "go-getter" or the "livewire", not those of the "successful smilers the city can use"; "keen types" are mistrusted. Whatever one does, horizons are likely to be limited; in any case, working-class people add quickly, money doesn't seem to make people happier, nor does power' (p. 67).

This lack of interest in social mobility, manifest across the class as a whole, goes together with a sharp sense of 'us' versus 'them' – 'them' being those in positions of power, whether it be the workplace shop steward, members of the 'higher' professions, or politicians. The key point, as Hoggart sees it, is that working-class social identity is deeply marked by what, academically, can be called dialectical opposition: the working class identifies itself in and through opposition to those possessing significant material means, social prestige and decision-making powers. Restriction to a small-scale locale and little desire for social mobility amount to a pronounced sense of difference towards members of other classes: 'The question of how we face "Them" (whoever "They" are) is, at last, the question of how we stand in relation to anything not visibly and intimately part of our local universe. The working-class splitting of the world into "Us" and

"Them" is on this side a symptom of their difficulty in meeting abstract or general questions' (p. 85).

Part of the polemical aspect of Hoggart's analysis is expressed as a desire to correct what he sees as a stereotypical overemphasis on those members of the working class consciously attempting to overcome class-based social restrictions. While he acknowledges the historical role of politically conscious working-class struggle, he sees self-satisfaction and complacency as key attributes of the majority working-class culture. It should be recalled that Hoggart wrote his book as the British 'angry young men' phenomenon – captured, iconically, in the character of Jimmy Porter in John Osborne's 1956 play *Look Back in Anger* – was attracting widespread popular attention and establishing the figure of the dissatisfied working-class individual as a cultural cliché.

While Hoggart's book, in its second part in particular, is suffused with a sense of impending crisis for British working-class culture, it insists that championing a rise to political consciousness for the class as whole is untenable. If anything, Hoggart errs in the opposite direction and depicts the working class as all too easily duped into 'false consciousness'. Ultimately, however, the power of Hoggart's book lies in its precarious balance between celebration and criticism of British working-class culture. Drawing from my own experience, I recognize the continued salience of Hoggart's analysis. At the local comprehensive school I attended, for example, there was very little desire to do particularly well in final exams, let alone to go on to some prestigious university. As secondary-school students, in general our horizons and aspirations were strictly limited and our political consciousness hardly developed at all. Tory politicians amounted to figures of reflexive contempt but we hardly felt they were part of our life, residing as they were in a shadowy and distant southern capital city.

Given our focus here on contemporary populism and the underlying argument I am advancing in this book as to its causes, the working-class attitude towards the political class is of key interest. As noted, Hoggart's British working class is characterized by an ingrained distrust of all figures of authority. He remarks in the preface of his book that 'one of the most striking and ominous features of our present cultural situation is the division between the technical languages of the experts and the extraordinarily low level of the organs of mass communication' (2009: xxx). This speaks to a basic concern of the communicative divide between rulers and ruled. In other words, it is essentially a problem of democratic culture. If the manner and means in which a democracy is administered to all intents and purposes make up a world quite different to that inhabited by the majority of the enfranchised, then there can be little prospect that the lived experience of the working class will entail any plausible sense of self-rule. Hoggart's chief concern, then, could be interpreted as the absence of the lived experience of democracy within the British working class.

To understand better this lack of democratic experience among the working class we need to reflect more on what Hoggart has to say about the Us/Them separation. Hoggart does not see the typical working-class attitude as one of envy directed towards the rich and influential. If anything, the actual attitude is one of sympathy and pity: money and fame don't appear to make people any happier, so it's best not to chase after them. This guarded and sceptical attitude towards members of outside classes is simply the flipside of the restricted scale and intimacy of working-class life. As Hoggart remarks: 'The world of "Them" is the world of the bosses, whether those bosses are private individuals, or as is increasingly the case today, public officials. "Them" may be, as occasion requires, anyone from the classes outside other than the few individuals from those classes whom working-people know as individuals' (2009: 57). The concreteness of working-class life means that it basically amounts to a face-to-face community, beyond which nothing can be taken too seriously.

This collective attitude, in the context of contemporary neoliberal political culture, would undoubtedly be condemned as lacking in personal 'aspiration'. Leftist critique could also, albeit more sympathetically, dismiss this attitude as a symptom of 'internalized oppression' or as indicating a lack of self-affirming agency. The neoliberal dispensation has become so all-pervasive that lack of personal ambition closely resembles an original sin. In Hoggart's account, the working class is depicted as largely drawn to the 'superstitions' of fortune and luck, rather than to social advancement based on personal ambition: 'To working-class people, luck figures as importantly and naturally as steady endeavour or brains or beauty; it is as much an attribute you have to accept. They are prepared to admire these other qualities, but give as much importance to the sheer chance of having luck with you' (p. 119).

Overall, it is difficult not to feel acute ambivalence about Hoggart's analysis of the British working class. On the one hand, it possesses undoubted integrity thanks to being drawn from personal experience and an obvious attitude of sympathetic understanding. On the other hand, it is easy to suspect that Hoggart's more critical comments play on time-honoured conservative myths of the 'lower orders' as half-witted yokels with only a confused sense of the broader world existing beyond their immediate community. To his credit, Hoggart could see the coming storm all too clearly: a rapid increase in the communications and entertainment sectors which would profoundly affect Britain's post-war social fabric. Unlike Williams, whose work we shall consider in the next section, Hoggart largely avoids sketching out a desirable set of changes that could work to overcome the experienced gulf between the 'Us' of immediate working-class experience and the 'Them' who are essentially running the show.

As the second half of his book makes clear, part of Hoggart's reticence to outline a progressive future stems from a worry that the prevailing efforts to 'improve' the British working class have really amounted to substituting authentic working-class virtues with a degraded and diminished version of 'upper class' values and mores. Any amount of increased access to formal education, for example, will have 'little compensatory bearing on the fact that concurrent changes are bringing about increased trivialization in productions for the majority' (2009: 307). Contemporary entertainment media are, he affirms, 'full of a corrupt brightness, of improper appeals and moral evasions' (p. 308). While authentic working-class life gains its colour through concrete personal intimacy, commercialized products of mass entertainment 'tend towards uniformity' (p. 309).

Hoggart's concerns about cultural uniformity, interestingly, echo an older argument advanced by a classic liberal such as John Stuart Mill (1989) in his influential essay *On Liberty*, published in 1859. But whereas for Mill liberty was largely a matter of the rights of the individual set over and against the collective pressures of society, Hoggart (2009) portrays working-class life as a matter of intrinsically shared existence. More specifically, what worried Hoggart in the late 1950s was the increasing tendency, made possible by advances in communications technology, to confront members of the working class with confected images of themselves. To Hoggart's mind, this had the potential to hollow out authentic working-class culture from the inside by rendering individuals reflexively self-conscious rather than spontaneous.

While, on the surface, appealing to a class's desire for media representation might appear to be an act of empowerment, in reality this could be seen as inducing a traumatic splitting of the working-class self-image. More straightforwardly, it could be said that the working class was now, for the first time in its history, being systematically confronted with an image of itself constructed by those existing outside its class boundaries. It is clear, based on Hoggart's (2009) analysis, that he regarded the sense of a tight-knit community as the principal salient feature of working-class life. As Hoggart experienced at first hand in northern England in the 1930s and 1940s, the reality of such a life is made up of everyday encounters with neighbours and family who remain constantly close at hand. The limitedness and self-satisfaction of working-class life were profoundly disrupted by the rise of popular media in the post-Second World War period, as the 'consumer society' took hold in the 1950s and 1960s. Such developments threatened to undo the legacy of earlier working-class struggles for political representation and enfranchisement. To further understand how contemporary populism arose, we need to explore in more depth how this shift from collective empowerment to individualized consumerism played out.

Williams and the unfinished democratic revolution

The underlying argument of this book, let us recall, is that contemporary populism is a consequence of the gradual neoliberal disempowerment of the working class in the context of liberal democratic politics. As the sense of distance between the concerns of most of the governed and the governing class has deepened over the last four decades, the result has been growing working-class resignation and eventual anger at the increasing sense of powerlessness. This is consistent with Hoggart's (2009) characterization of traditional British working-class attitudes towards politicians in terms of scepticism, cynicism and an overall sense that members of the governing class are 'in it for themselves'. Accordingly, shifting and increasingly unpredictable party-political loyalties on the part of the working class are best understood as a clear sign that the neoliberalization of democratic politics now appears all but irreversible to working-class voters. Following this line of analysis, contemporary populism is better grasped as the consequence rather than cause of a crisis in a democratic political culture.

In the first chapter of this book, I introduced Raymond Williams's idea of the 'long revolution'. In this chapter, I want to elaborate on it by reconstructing Williams's original context and argument. In *Culture and Society* (1958) Williams offers an interpretation of British literature from the Romantic period in which he sees it as a gradual recognition and representation of working-class consciousness. According to his narrative, the politics of modern British culture gave rise to various forms of containing and controlling this process of working-class identity and social recognition. This politics first became overt when the British working class started to claim a certain autonomy for itself from the 1830s on.

The important thing to note, from Williams's perspective, is that this process of working-class self-representation was constantly dynamic and culturally contested. In nineteenth-century British cultural criticism a dominant middle class of reviewers and essayists established a position according to which popular democratic politics was either intrinsically antithetical to a civilized society or could only be rendered acceptable by a thoroughgoing cultural education. In either case, working-class values were to be transformed by elevating them to the status of a properly civilized worldview. In the most dramatic way of formulating the argument of orthodox Victorian thinking, there was simply no such thing as 'working-class culture' – the very idea was a contradiction in terms.

Educational reform, understood in this patronizing manner, was grasped as the prerequisite of political reform: prior to being politically empowered, the working class needed to be culturally enlightened and thereby socially improved as a preparation for proper political agency. Many powerful political and cultural figures of Victorian Britain – Thomas Carlyle's (2010) anti-democratic polemics from the mid-nineteenth century are a case in point – regarded this whole task as quite hopeless and saw the working class as beyond the pale of radical improvement. Contesting this long-established cultural critique of popular sovereignty, in *The Long Revolution* (1961) Williams advances a set of concrete demands for a progressive democratic future in Britain. Reading these demands at the present juncture, sixty years later, puts into relief the current democratic deficit of British society and politics two decades into the twenty-first century.

After initially stressing how the democratic 'revolution' is at a very early stage of development, Williams underscores how the social process involved ultimately requires a novel understanding of human life and flourishing: 'The long revolution, which is now at the centre of our history, is not for democracy as a political system alone, nor for the equitable distribution of more products, nor for general access to the means of learning and communication. Such changes, difficult enough in themselves, derive meaning and direction, finally, from new conceptions of man and society which many have worked to describe and interpret' (1961: 121). Williams is here describing the socialist inheritance and the attendant effort to think beyond the alienations and deprivations of industrial capitalism. In the current context, the most important element of this description is his insistence that the democratization of economic production and political decision-making are ultimately mere means through which a radical social and cultural transformation is to be achieved.

As Williams saw only too well, under capitalism economic liberalization is generally offered as a surrogate for social emancipation. The accompanying mantra is: free the markets and you will be set free. The rejection of this equation lies, of course, at the heart of all variants of socialism. In this connection it is important to point out that Williams, as a leading member of the British New Left, rejects the fundamental economism that was standard practice for socialist orthodoxy throughout the first half of the twentieth century. Against this, he centres his idea of socialism on the goal of achieving generalized autonomy in relation to the immediate material conditions of everyday life: 'If socialism accepts the distinction of "work" from "life", which has then to be written off as "leisure" and "personal interests"; if it sees politics as "government", rather than as a process of common decision and administration ... it is simply a late form of capitalist politics, or just the more efficient organization of human beings around a system of industrial production' (1961: 113–14). In other words, socialism, for Williams, is ultimately about attaining generalized material autonomy as a source of collective well-being, rather than a matter of achieving a more efficient rationalization in relation to the economy.

What is most striking and salient to our general discussion here is that, for Williams, it is socialism alone – rather than capitalism – that provides an adequate political vision for a truly democratic culture. It is precisely this insight that neoliberalism – with its counter that only capitalism and not socialism offers the material basis for a democratic society – has succeeded in rendering marginal and largely discredited since the early 1980s. In this connection, we might recall, from the previous chapter, the struggle of the skilled artisan class of the nineteenth century to attain control over the conditions of their work practice. This can be viewed, of course, as merely self-interested economic protectionism. With recourse to Williams's interpretation of socialism, by contrast, this drive for control is really a matter of working-class dignity achieved by means of material autonomy. In other words, it goes beyond any relative economic improvement and becomes a matter of being recognized on one's own terms as a producer of social value.

In the context of the present book, the stance on contemporary populism advanced here is granted crucial coherence and direction by Williams's conception of the decisive connections between the growth of working-class political consciousness and the rise of modern democratic culture. This connection, I believe, offers us a meaningful gauge by which to measure the current state of British democracy. Part of Williams's critique here relates to the impoverished language and imagery at our disposal for capturing the truly radical nature of the modern democratic project: 'The symbols of democracy, in the English mind, are as likely to be institutions of power and antiquity, such as the Palace of Westminster, as the active process of popular decision, such as a committee or jury. A more decisive social image came from the other part of this movement: the rise of economic individualism' (1961: 104).

While it may seem innocuous enough, referencing the *Palace* of Westminster as the democratic 'mother of parliaments' elicits a troublingly equivocal image. Palaces, we learn as children, contain kings and queens, princes and princesses; the people are not really present at all except as humble servants. The clear implication in this is that politics essentially goes on not in the everyday lives of the working class, but rather in the elaborate and arcane workings of another class in another place. In addition, Williams also points to the resultant image of democracy produced by the 'bourgeois' revolution, namely economic and social upward mobility. Williams's reference to the dominant discourse and imagery pertaining to modern democracy is crucial, I believe, as it points to limits of the political imagination that have been further restricted by the ensuing decades of neoliberal governance.

This separation of form and substance becomes the keynote of the final section of Williams's *The Long Revolution*, which offers a kind of social-cultural 'state of the nation' enquiry. He writes: 'Our main trouble now is that we have many of the forms of democracy, but find these continually confused by the tactics of those who do not really believe in it, who are genuinely afraid of common decisions openly arrived at, and who have unfortunately partly succeeded in weakening the patterns of feeling of democracy which alone could substantiate the institutions' (1961: 308).

What Williams is questioning here is the extent to which a truly democratic culture is securely embedded in British society. Then, as now, 'the people' are predominantly seen as tragically incompetent at knowing and facilitating their own best interests. In other words, a patrician bias runs through the heart of British democratic culture. One might think that since 1961, when Williams's book was published, Britain would have developed a genuinely popular political culture. While it is certainly true that images of the working class in such contexts as 'reality TV' proliferate as never before, at a deeper level it seems clear that the cultural process of democratization has been in reverse for many decades.

A key element of Williams's vision of a truly democratic social order is characterized by the material overcoming of the dichotomy between work and non-working existence. As in our own times, in the late 1950s and early 1960s there was much concern about the social costs of work expressed by authors with starkly different political sentiments. Daniel Bell's *Work and Its Discontents* (1956), Hannah Arendt's *The Human Condition* (2018 [1958]) and Henri Lefebvre's *Critique of Everyday Life: Volume II* (2002 [1961]) are examples of this. Against this backdrop, Williams's (1961) preoccupation with the same issue is easier to account for. Again, for him the problem is the non-voluntary nature of work, the fact that it represents the material manifestation of a generalized lack of autonomy under advanced capitalism: 'The integration of work and life, and the inclusion of the activities we call cultural in the ordinary social organization, are the basic terms of an alternative form of society. In their light, the system of decision becomes something more than the traditional version of politics; it necessarily includes, for example, control over the direction and nature of our labour' (1961: 113).

In light of Williams's concern with work and autonomy, one can view the contemporary neoliberal condition, with its 'sharing economy', as a kind of generalized simulation of the democratic future envisaged by Williams in the early 1960s. As Angela McRobbie adroitly analyses it in her book *Be Creative: Making a Living in the New Culture Industries* (2016), neoliberal ideology makes a universal appeal to workers to see themselves as a kind of entrepreneurial artist. While this may bring a certain glamour and consolation to a twenty-something art student eking out a meagre living, as the need for economic security becomes more pressing, self-promotional freelancing all too often leads to a relentless treadmill of drudgery and precarity.

I highlight these recent developments in neoliberal patterns of work as Williams is convinced that control over work conditions is a crucial litmus test of democratic culture. The less work looks and feels likes something the majority of people decide on to advance their collective interests but rather as something imposed on them as a largely uncontrolled environmental factor, the less we can claim a society is truly democratic. As Williams notes: 'It is difficult to feel that we are really governing ourselves if in so central a part of our living as our work most of us have no share in decisions that immediately affect us' (1961: 306).

Workplace democracy is, of course, an archetypal concern of socialist thinking. In the final chapter of this book, I will critique the growing consensus, on the left and the right, that we are facing an 'end of work' crisis precipitated by the latest wave of technology-driven automation. The idea that work will, for the majority, be a thing of the past within a generation or so ignores the fact that 'bullshit jobs' (see Graeber 2018) already exist in their millions in the most advanced economies. The 'end of work' thesis largely sidesteps the challenges of democratic culture, as taking work out of the equation offers an obvious positive way forward for a democratically controlled economy. At best, it simply shifts the central concern to the classic Marxist issue of 'ownership of the means of production'. One thing is sufficiently clear on this score already: the 'platform' capitalism of Uber, Airbnb and the like is not the emancipating nirvana it is generally portrayed as being and represents, instead, a nadir of collective worker control over the organization of productive work.

A final point to be drawn from Williams's account of democratic culture relates to the importance of education. Williams's formative experience as a teacher in adult education colleges in the 1950s is clearly in play when he remarks: 'It was only very slowly, and then only in the sphere of adult education, that the working class, drawing indeed on very old intellectual traditions and on important dissenting elements in the English educational tradition, made its contribution to the modern educational debate' (1961: 144). Williams is here alluding to the long tradition of self-education, in the predominant form of night schools in Britain in the nineteenth century. In this domain, Williams is generally more sanguine than Hoggart was about the empowering potential of formal education for the working class. But Williams's optimism on this score carries a crucial proviso: educators of the working class should be directly acquainted with the realities of working-class life. Otherwise, the principal task of formal education is liable to be that 'improving' cultural mission articulated by the likes of Matthew Arnold in the mid-Victorian period.

Once again, we can measure how far below the democratic ideal a society stands when considering the contemporary condition of education. While secondary schooling, particularly in the US (see Ravitch, 2014, 2016), has become increasingly preoccupied with bureaucratic accountability by means of standardized testing and school league tables, university education in the UK has come to be predominantly seen as a lucrative sector of the domestic economy (see Collini, 2018). The cultural capital enjoyed by Britain's universities brings British students into direct competition with young adults from wealthy families in 'developing' economies. With record levels of remuneration for college vice chancellors making the newspaper headlines on a regular basis (Adams, 2019) and dire warnings that the UK is rapidly following the disastrous lead of the US into unsustainable levels of student debt, it would be hard to make the case that Britain's universities are charging ahead at the vanguard of a democratic revolution. According to a 2020 report by the UK government, debt levels of students in England stood at £140 billion by March 2020, are predicted to reach a cumulative total of £560 billion by mid-century, with only 25 per cent of students likely to repay loans in full (UK Parliament, 2020).

I draw attention here to the state of contemporary work and education in the UK in order to establish a gauge for the true state of where the country stands relative to Williams's conception of democratic culture. For Williams, as shown, such culture turns on how much control people have over the material conditions of their everyday lives. Dramatically sharpened inequalities of wealth and income in liberal democracies such as the UK have been accompanied by significant erosion of workplace unionization and other means of worker control. Finally, the imperative that a majority of people enter post-secondary education in order to secure a well-paid and relatively stable job is increasingly burdening students from working-class households with unsustainable levels of debt. In the next section, we consider an additional set of burdens faced by the contemporary working class – in the form of social and cultural denigration.

The rise and fall of the working class

This chapter deals with what I am calling the 'invention of working-class culture'. By 'invention' I mean an overt conceptualization rather than a material creation. Clearly, the British working class did not first appear on the scene in the 1950s; but it was at this point in time that a strategic assertion of British working-class culture came to the fore through poplar media with a hitherto unknown level of force and reach. Due to the fact that the very mention of the 'working class' is something of an anathema in contemporary politics, it becomes necessary to reflect on how the word 'class' came to be used in historical development. Early on in *The Long Revolution* Williams gets to grips with the social and linguistic history of the word 'class' and remarks:

> A particular and crucial addition was the concept of 'class', which is quite different from the static concepts of 'order' and 'rank' because it includes this kind of middle term between 'the individual' and 'society' – the individual relates to his society through his class. Yet 'class' carries an emphasis different from 'community' or 'association', because it is not a face-to-face grouping, but, like 'society' itself, an abstraction. (1961: 78)

Williams also points out that, right through the eighteenth and into the early nineteenth century, leading voices in British politics ascribed a pejorative sense to the term 'democracy' as synonymous with mob rule. This 'hatred of democracy', in Rancière's phrase, was thus a clear inheritance involved in the inception of modern British liberal democracy. In the post-Second World War era of unparalleled Western economic growth, the electorate could not be so readily rejected as an unruly mob. Instead they started to be seen (and see themselves) in terms of a more or less passively aggregated 'consumer demand'. Consumption could then be embraced as the great social leveller, a largely rhetorical act of equality that has only intensified over the decades since Williams published his book. In this atmosphere, the very invocation of class precipitates an adverse reaction. Williams notes the denigration of class politics in the early 1960s: 'But the stage has been reached when the emphasis on class has been seen as the most obvious denial of brotherhood, and when resentments against an existing or remembered class situation have been massively transferred to those who continue to talk about class' (1961: 108–9). Thus, where socialism hopes that class consciousness will unite, under neoliberalism it is sure to be presented as something that divides.

These phenomena of social anxiety and antagonism brought about by the categories of class lie at the heart of a key study published by Richard Sennett and Jonathan Cobb, *The Hidden Injuries of Class* (1972). Sennett and Cobb's reflections on the politics of the working class in Boston in the US offer a very valuable extension of the analysis presented here. While Hoggart (2009) and Williams (1958) consider the British working class at a moment when there are only faint traces of the neoliberal counter-revolution to come, the American study reports on workers who are clearly in the throes of early neoliberalization. Although there are, of course, many salient and crucial differences between British and American social history, what I want to focus on here is the profound *ambivalence* towards upward social mobility expressed by the working-class subjects interviewed by Sennett and Cobb.

This ambivalence takes the form of feeling compelled to overcome the trappings and markers of working-class identity (most obviously, a blue-collar job), while at the same time refusing to identify personally with any 'superior' position attained. As Sennett and Cobb (1972) portray it, the working class in the United States finds itself trapped in a no-win situation: either a person stays put in a traditional working-class social position and feels a sense of social failure; or they transcend their class origins only to feel they are now doing something such as white-collar office work that doesn't amount to a 'real' job. A similar phenomenon arises between the generations of a working-class family, where the father will work harder in his blue-collar job in order to enable his children to overcome their class origins. As a result, that father may well start to see himself as unworthy in the eyes of his upwardly mobile offspring.

The central contribution of Sennett and Cobb's (1972) study is its acute social psychology of class. This is in large part due to the methodology they selected: extended interviews conducted with their subjects over a period of time. As university researchers, they are acutely aware of the cultural capital they possess in the eyes of their interviewees. This brings an internal class dynamic to their whole investigation and produces very valuable insights into class-based anxiety on the part of their interviewees themselves. While this might have led their working-class subjects to be very guarded and reserved during interviews, the youth of the investigators and the fact that Sennett himself grew up in an urban working-class community gives rise to some revelatory moments of exchange. Early on, Sennett and Cobb (1972) attempt to evoke what might be described as the social atmosphere in which their subjects live out their day-to-day lives.

The overall tenor of this amounts to pervasive social anxiety: 'This fear of being summoned before some hidden bar of judgment and being found inadequate infects the lives of people who are coping perfectly well from day to day; it is a matter of a hidden weight, a hidden anxiety, in the *quality* of experience, a matter of feeling inadequately in control where an observer making material calculations would conclude the workingman had adequate control' (Sennett and Cobb, 1972: 33–4). This anxiety, it is found, stems from a felt need to demonstrate ability in a socially validating way: 'That ability is the badge of individual worth, that calculations of ability create an image of a few individuals standing out from the mass, that to be an individual by virtue of ability is to have the right to transcend one's social origins – these are the basic suppositions of a society that produces feelings of powerlessness and inadequacy' (p. 62). As Sennett and Cobb see it, American workers regard themselves as caught up in a competition for social dignity that gives them no rest. Even when they have attained such social esteem through recognized ability they are likely to ascribe this elevation as much to luck as to hard work and personal virtue. Either way, those with true 'ability' can only ever be a small minority separated out from the mass.

Sennett and Cobb see the class structure in America as a mechanism for transforming a general desire for freedom into social indignity. While they clearly acknowledge that this structure affects everyone, they insist that the injuries of class apply pre-eminently to the working class: 'The position we take in this book is that everyone in this society, rich and poor, plumber and professor, is subject to a scheme of values that tells him he must validate the self in order to win others' respect and his own. When the plumber makes this attempt, however, the feelings involved are quite different than when a professor does it' (1972: 75). Sennett and Cobb explicitly reference Hoggart's (2009) *Uses of Literacy* as 'a beautiful evocation of the feeling among laborers that we are unfree, but dignified in our oppression because we have each other' (1972: 29). This raises for them the question why, in the case of the workers they interviewed, there was a clear sense that 'their dignity is on the line' (p. 29).

Their explanation for the difference references the distinct experience of the nineteenth-century European immigrant: competition from within a constantly replenished pool of unskilled labourers, a lack of worker organization, and, finally, having recourse to inward-looking ethnic enclaves that effectively blocked any sense of unity as members of the American working class more generally. But recall that, according to Hoggart (2009), the British working class is also focused on family and neighbourhood. Recall also that, as Williams points out, class entails an abstraction relative to face-to-face community. While Hoggart recorded his experience of a British working class for whom 'solidarity is helped by the lack of scope for the growth of ambition' (Hoggart, 2009: 66), Sennett and Cobb reveal an American working class pressured, at every turn, with expectations of social improvement.

While all of the factors of American social history identified by Sennett and Cobb no doubt played a role, it is possible to recognize, looking back over the last five decades, signs of the early stages of a shift to the neoliberal social and cultural paradigm. As David Harvey (2005) ably demonstrates, this shift was anything but spontaneous but rather involved consciously concerted efforts to push back against the powerful American counterculture movement of the 1960s. The year after Sennett and Cobb's book was published is generally recognized as the year neoliberalism came onto the scene in an overtly political manner, with the Chilean coup of October 1973 (see Harvey, 2005: 39–40). A month later, the oil crisis brought about by OPEC's (Organization of the Petroleum Exporting Countries) restriction of oil supply precipitated a global economic slowdown that would not be effectively altered until the arrival of the overtly neoliberal political regimes and accompanying economic policies of the late 1970s and early 1980s (pp. 26–7).

Harvey also draws attention to the bankruptcy and fiscal restructuring of New York City in 1975 (2005: 44–6). This heralded, we can now see in retrospect, a massive shift away from manufacturing towards construction and financial sectors on the part of the wealthiest economies. Along the way, mass unemployment and a relentless drive for efficiency and workforce 'flexibility' allowed government at every level to discipline workers and push through anti-union measures (pp. 52–3). By the early 1980s, with the ascendency of Thatcher and Reagan, business schools attained a higher profile at leading US universities, allowing them to alter the intellectual and social milieu on college campuses. At the same time, popularizers of neoliberalism such as Milton Friedman reached millions with their books and television programmes (Harvey, 2005: 44). In sum, the decade between 1973 and 1982 bore witness to an epoch-making shift in the political conjuncture, the long-term effects of which we are living through today.

Returning to the analysis of the social attitudes among Boston's working-class community by Sennett and Cobb (1972), we are able to reframe what they encountered at the time in light of the transition to neoliberal governance sketched above. The main thesis of Sennett and Cobb's book is expressed in their title, namely that class identities involve 'hidden injuries': 'hidden', because class is a structural rather than personal social reality, operating largely below the threshold of personal consciousness; 'injuries', because the class system fragments those who have to operate on its terms, making them feel unfulfilled and unworthy whatever they do and whatever goals they work towards.

In contrast to the presentation of the same issues in Hoggart (2009) and Williams (1958), one gets little sense of pride in their working-class identity on the part of the American workers interviewed by Sennett and Cobb (1972). Instead, these workers seem caught in the very trap Williams alludes to time and again: namely, that the working class has no culture of its own and 'culture' is only ever something to be attained by overcoming working-class origins. As Sennett and Cobb report of their interviewees: 'For them, history is challenging them and their children to become "cultured," in the intellectual's sense of that word, if they want to achieve respect in the new American terms; and toward that challenge they feel deeply ambivalent' (1972: 18).

Speaking of one interviewed subject, they observe: 'Capturing respect in the larger America, then, means to Frank getting into an educated position; but capturing that respect means that he no longer respects himself. This contradiction ran through every discussion we held, as an image either of what people felt compelled to do with their own lives or of what they sought for their sons' (pp. 22–3). In other words, the way to gain value as a member of the working class in America involves acknowledging that one is, to begin with, intrinsically worthless. Gaining value is thus a transition out of worthlessness. At the same time, most who strive to gain this value will fail: 'In these struggles for worth there are two classes, the many and the few; the selves of the many are in limbo, the selves of the few who have performed win respect. But the few need the many: individuals exist only so long as the mass exists, a point of reference consisting of others who seem pretty much alike' (p. 67). In other words, all working-class individuals are caught up in an effort to prove themselves that depends, inevitably, on the failure in this effort for the majority.

This recalls Hoggart's (2009) observations of the British working-class embrace of chance as a mechanism of social mobility. While the means of social mobility are, ostensibly, ability and perseverance, members of the working class have a deeply held belief that socially acknowledged success is, in reality, a magical process predicated on sheer good luck. Luck is something a person has that cannot be deployed in a controlled way. This is a narrative framed, of course, to capture the fact that the class structures in which worth is to be proven are beyond the control of the working class as whole. Class society is, so to speak, a dialogue where the working class listen to their betters. It is not, above all, anything like an equal exchange. If it were, then members outside of the working class would, to some extent at least, feel compelled to aspire to typically working-class attributes and lifestyles.

In Sennett and Cobb's analysis, class works in a way akin to Foucault's 1975 book *Discipline and Punish* (1995) with its notion of disciplinary systems that operate by having the subject held to account through constant testing by an external authority. The system is successfully installed when such subjects internalize this sense of monitoring, thereby subjecting themselves to the once externally imposed disciplinary voice or gaze. This creates a curious social dynamic, according to which those in the working class are primarily responsible for their own sense of social inadequacy. The general experience this precipitates in the working class is that the social system is a swindle, the negative effects of which fall on members of their class: 'The badges of inner ability people wear seem, in sum, unfairly awarded – yet hard to repudiate. That is the injury of class, in day-to-day experience, that the people we encountered face; it is a tangled relationship of denied freedom and dignity infinitely more complicated than a resentment of "what other people are doing to me"' (Sennett and Cobb, 1972: 118).

In this astute observation we can see the social origins of a long-standing working-class resentment of the political and social system that has arguably borne fruit in the form of contemporary populism. If accepted, this analysis would be in accord with the main argument advanced in this book, namely that contemporary populism should be seen as a long-term effect of long-term working-class 'injuries' and indignities suffered under decades of neoliberal capitalism. Sennett and Cobb (1972), in common with Hoggart's (2009) earlier analysis, accentuate the fact that the lives of working-class people are pervaded by the sense that the social rules they are obliged to work under are rigged against them; that gaining social prestige is akin to playing at a roulette wheel where everything is set against their winning and weighted in favour of the casino managers. The key difference between the two accounts is that Hoggart (2009) is able to recall an earlier British working-class culture of the 1930s and 1940s that inherited an inner resilience against the snares of the class system. We might dismiss this resilience as nothing better than collective sour grapes – we can't have what they have, so we don't want it – but Hoggart makes a strong case that the virtues of working-class life are positive cases of social authenticity.

Sennett and Cobb's interviewees, by contrast, seem incapable of adopting this defensive posture. Not to play the game, even while one is conscious of the likelihood of failing, is just not an option. Again, like Hoggart (2009), the American researchers consider the distinction between 'worthy' and 'unworthy' members of the working class. While Hoggart accentuates good family values, the ability to hold down a job, and avoiding excessive consumption of alcohol, Sennett and Cobb focus on the spectre of those members of the working class who draw on welfare benefits: 'Those who refuse to sacrifice must therefore be the incarnation of evil, the denial of *anything* a decent man does, evil not simply unto themselves, but destroyers of his own powers to believe and hope ... It is for this reason that hard-working fathers are both appalled and fascinated by the figure of the "welfare chiseller"' (Sennett and Cobb, 1972: 138).

Due to the sense among the working class that their value is not recognized by those possessing a higher-class status, their only immediate source of worth is the negative one of not being a welfare recipient. We hear an echo of this defensive posture when contemporary politicians, always keen to avoid reference to the working class, make laudatory allusions to 'hard-working families'. What we find here, therefore, is a mass psychology of the working class that is based not so much on the aspiration to transcend one's class status but rather on an anxiety that one will no longer be able to provide for oneself and one's family through work. What that work does for the self-development and intrinsic worth of the worker is not considered a matter of primary importance. This makes evident, as Sennett and Cobb (1972) see it, the cardinal virtue of sacrifice operating within working-class life.

The discreet charms of the working class

In conjunction, the work of Hoggart (2009), Williams (1958, 1961) and Sennett and Cobb (1972) allows us a way to grasp the meaning of working-class culture. These studies, of course, pertain to the condition of the working class in the UK and US two generations ago. They could therefore be readily dismissed as of little to no direct relevance to contemporary society and politics. Why, then, have recourse to these classic accounts of working-class life in an analysis of the current wave of populism? The answer to the question is twofold: first, the obfuscations of four decades of neoliberal ideology make necessary a retrieval of the positive meaning of working-class culture; and, second, I contend that the problem of social value through work – the central problem of socialist thinking – remains a central issue for current politics.

Recall the fundamental argument advanced in this book, namely that contemporary populism has arisen as a result of a crisis in democratic culture precipitated by the protracted history of neoliberal governance since the late 1970s/early 1980s. As argued in the previous chapter, the historical origins of democracy in the UK (and elsewhere) reside in the various workers' movements of the nineteenth century and their struggle for control over the material conditions of everyday life. This struggle can be seen through two principal lenses: on the one hand, in terms of a demand for formal political powers such as the vote and for the improvement of workplace conditions including higher wages, a shortened work-week and so forth; on the other hand, in terms of recognition for working-class cultural values. The position of the working class in places like the UK has significantly worsened on both fronts as the scope and depth of neoliberalization has increased. Following this line of argument, in the first decades of the twenty-first century populism has arisen as a widespread political sentiment in reaction to this generations-long diminution of working-class social power and standing.

It is tempting, by contrast, to take a much shorter-term view of contemporary populism and see it as stemming largely from the austerity politics ushered in as a result of the Great Recession which began in 2008. My argument, however, is that the visible populism that resulted, in 2016, in the Brexit referendum result in the UK and the presidential election victory of Donald Trump in the US are long-range epiphenomena of a fifty-year-long process of inexorable neoliberalization. Thus, I am arguing here for a much longer view, one that goes back at least as far as the origins of the neoliberal counter-revolution beginning in the early 1970s. Since then, the political voice of the working class in Britain (and in the United States) has been weakened to a point of virtual silence. Without a coherent sense of political praxis as was offered by the nineteenth-century heritage of socialism, members of the working class are presented with a stark choice: play the game of dignity acquisition established by neoliberal capitalism or be subject to more or less complete social opprobrium or oblivion.

While 'dropping out' acquired a certain cachet in the counter-culture of the 1960s, this was arguably never a perspective credible to the majority of the British working class. For my own parents, who came of age in 1950s Liverpool, the counter-culture might as well have existed on another planet as they left the city and started a family in the long shadow of post-war austerity. I came of age in the 1980s, a time when mass unemployment and anti-union political sentiments were the norm. There was a certain counter-culture opposed to Thatcherism at this time, but it was largely expressed in the cultural terms of music and the arts rather than overt political activism. To hear Morrissey sing 'England is mine, and it owes me a living' sounded rebellious on some level to my 14-year-old self, but I didn't find myself in the fug of the local Labour Club the following week. Looking back, my own childhood contained many remnants of the northern working-class life so effectively evoked by Hoggart: the close family connections, restricted sense of neighbourhood scale, animated personalized narratives and playful rejection of authority.

Though unconscious of it at the time, I was clearly and thoroughly inducted into working-class culture. And my 'escape' followed the route taken by Hoggart, Williams and Sennett, namely into higher education. But, from a British perspective at least, my own path through academia already seems embarrassingly antiquated compared to the contemporary reality of over £9,000 a year in university tuition fees. I, by contrast, paid nothing for tuition and was given a maintenance grant by my local education authority. This change is just one illustrative symptom of the consolidation of neoliberalism in Britain. While the 1980s was a decade of slash and burn, where the application of a 'shock doctrine' (Klein, 2007) to domestic politics was everywhere evident, in the 1990s British neoliberalism came of age and succeeded in presenting to the voting public a less abrasive, seemingly more caring and progressive, countenance.

After almost two decades out of power, the British Labour Party had, by the time it formed a government under Tony Blair in 1997, brought itself into line with the new neoliberal orthodoxy. Weakening its links with the trade union movement out of which it had been formed in the late nineteenth and early twentieth centuries, Blair's 'Third Way' politics indulged in a 'beyond left and right' rhetoric that aspired to take Britain beyond 'Punch and Judy' oppositional politics. The only problem with this perspective is that it masks rather than articulates the real oppositions that exist in capitalist liberal democracies. Refusing to 'play the game' of class politics, in this case, meant that the major British party historically founded to further working-class interests had now abandoned that historical mission in an effort to capture the 'middle ground'.

As we saw in Chapter 1 when reviewing Mouffe's account, liberal democratic politics can only flourish when party plurality allows the heterogeneous interests present in capitalist societies to be given an effective voice. When all 'centre-ground' parties strive to occupy essentially the same political position, this confirms the working-class suspicion that politicians are really 'all the same' and simply 'in it for themselves'. The labour movement's party-political expression does not arise out of a narcissistic desire on the part of the working class to have politicians look and sound like themselves. Rather, it stems from a legitimate demand to have working-class interests credibly represented by democratically elected political representatives.

What the neoliberal order has brought about within liberal democracies is an attenuation of labour-based politics leading to a generalized sense that there is little to no genuine representation of working-class interests. The underlying formula of neoliberal governance involves making individuals responsible for their own economic welfare, while simultaneously undermining the social infrastructure that makes this collectively possible. As could be discerned already in the early 1970s by Sennett and Cobb (1972), members of the working class have become increasingly aware of being part of a social-economic mechanism that fatally wounds them but can neither be altered nor ignored. While mainstream politicians continue to speak the language of national interest, such interest coincides more and more with that of overseas investment on the part of huge multinational corporations. As Harvey has argued across multiple books (2005, 2010, 2012, 2014), neoliberalism is fundamentally about class domination by the tiny minority of billionaires over the majority working class. Such domination is fundamentally at odds with any genuinely democratic culture, where this is understood to entail the generalized ability to self-determine the material conditions of everyday life.

Having reconstructed a limited history of working-class politics and culture in the last two chapters, in the next two I turn to the state of politics in Britain towards the end of the second decade of the twenty-first century. In doing this the focus will be maintained on the realities of contemporary work under advanced neoliberalism, as it is arguably in the workplace that the deepest and most widely experienced impacts of neoliberal transformation have been felt. If 'working class' signifies a shared experience at least partly founded on the social realities of work, then it clearly follows that changing the conditions of work changes working-class experience. While it is important to avoid any temptation here to look back at earlier periods as the halcyon days of organized labour, the precipitous decline in trade union membership, both in Britain and in the US, is a clear indication of a weakened labour force. As Megan Dunn and James Walker note in a US Bureau of Labor Statistics report, 'the union membership rate was 20.1 percent in 1983 and declined to 11.1 percent in 2015' (Dunn and Walker, 2016: 2). A parallel trend in the UK was observed by Daniel Tomlinson in a 2017 report for the Resolution Foundation: 'There are now just 6.5 million people who are members of trade unions in the UK. This is down from 7 million at the start of this decade, and from a peak of 13 million in 1979.' Tomlinson concludes his assessment with this bleak prognosis: 'Without an embracing of new ways of working and finding new organisations to work with, trade unions might may well end up being a 20th century aberration.'

Neoliberal governance goes to great pains to reduce the effectiveness of union organization through more restrictive labour laws, more flexibility offered to employers and companies to hire and fire, media denigration of union leadership and so forth. Many younger workers in Britain and the United States today have had no experience of any union-protected workplace and consequently have only a vague notion of what good it might afford them and, more likely than not, an ill-defined sense that unions are obstacles rather than aids to workers' self-determination. Like the notion of the working class itself, neoliberal ideology perpetuates the idea that unions are some relict of the past. As we will examine in more detail in the next chapter when we turn to McRobbie's (2016) critique of the 'creative industries' touted in the UK since the early days of Blair's New Labour government, younger workers are enticed by the prospect of being their own boss, working in a fast-moving creative industry, and skipping from job to job as the only credible and desirable possibility in the labour market. More generally, in the next chapter we will consider how conceptions of valuable work are shaped under neoliberal capitalism. This will allow us to show how, in the wake of four decades of neoliberal governance, a definitive crisis in liberal democracy has been precipitated by the growing sense that the economy is not delivering anything like stability and equity to the vast majority of workers. It is in this context that contemporary populism must be placed if we want to both understand and move beyond it towards a genuinely progressive recasting of the political-economic order.

4

Work and the working class now

The denigration of the working class

In the previous chapter we considered the interpretation, offered by prominent cultural theorists and historians of the left, of the development and legacy of British working-class politics. Having a sense of this historical background is necessary, I believe, in order to gauge the social position of the British working class in recent decades. When I was born, in 1969, Britain was a considerably more economically equal country than it is today (see The Equality Trust, 2017). It seems intuitively plausible that higher levels of inequality would be likely to give rise to a sense of social and political disaffection among those who are worst off.

There is no doubt that profound wealth and income disparities generate a sense of resentment within a society. The analysis advanced in this book, however, accentuates a distinct underlying cause of populism, namely the sense of denigration suffered by the working class since the advent of neoliberal governance in the early 1980s. In other words, it is a problem of *social capital and recognition*. While a fairer distribution of income and wealth is no doubt a good thing in itself, as profoundly social beings an increase in material well-being cannot, I believe, compensate us for a significant lack of social recognition. This constitutes the 'hidden injury' highlighted in Sennett and Cobb's (1972) analysis of the Boston working class, which was considered in the previous chapter.

In this chapter, my focus is on the way attitudes towards the working class have changed, becoming increasingly negative as the shift to neoliberalism has hardened. On a fairly superficial level, this shift can be seen in the way British politicians, even in the Labour Party, have moved away from the very term 'working class'. Instead, we hear of 'hard-working families', the 'just about managing', and other largely euphemistic and vague epithets. As social historians are apt to point out, there has always been a tendency to symbolically separate out the 'deserving' poor from a subgroup that was considered feckless and unworthy of social support. The difference evident with the shift to neoliberalism in the early 1980s is that working-class values and lifestyles have been subject to a relentless campaign of cultural denigration. As Owen Jones points out in his book *Chavs*: 'The demonization of the working class cannot be understood without looking back at the Thatcherite experiment of the 1980s that forged the society we live in today' (2016: 40).

The question is how such denigration, practised over four decades, can be seen as a primary cause of the upsurge of populism in the UK in the twenty-first century. More specifically, how did British populism get channelled into the widespread animus against the European Union which precipitated the 2016 Brexit referendum result? When Britain joined the European Economic Community (EEC) in 1973, under a Conservative prime minister, it was in the immediate wake of empire and marked a certain acceptance of a post-imperial 'normalization' of Britain's standing within Europe. When, under a Labour government in 1975, the British people got their first chance to express the popular will through a referendum, two-thirds (67 per cent based on a national turnout of 65 per cent) voted in favour of continued membership (UK Parliament, 2013).

In the years preceding the 2016 referendum, the rise of the UK Independence Party (UKIP) constituted one of the most salient features of domestic party politics. Dominated by the personality of Nigel Farage, its leader from 2006, UKIP started to make inroads into Labour's traditional heartlands, securing close to a million votes in the general election of 2010 when Labour was defeated after being in power since 1997. A year earlier, UKIP had come second in the European elections. It then went on to poll 27.5 per cent at the 2014 European elections (thereby securing 24 MEPs), before gaining almost four million votes (a vote share of around 13 per cent) in the 2015 UK general election a year before the EU referendum (see Merrick, 2017).

Over the course of this electoral success, UKIP was able to capitalize on a working-class sense of abandonment by a business-friendly New Labour project, suspicion of bureaucracy and expert-led decision-making, and the nativism of English nationalism. Jones captures this conjunction with precision:

> The danger is of a savvy new populist right emerging, one that is comfortable talking about class and that offers reactionary solutions to working-class problems. It could denounce the demonization of the working class and the trashing of its identity. It could claim that the traditional party of working-class people, the Labour Party, has turned its back on them. Rather than focusing on the deep-seated economic issues that really underpin the grievances of working-class people, it could train its populist guns on immigration and cultural issues. (2016: 245–6)

Jones's basic argument is that, beginning with the rise of neoliberalism under Thatcher in the 1980s, the British working class has been subject to an increasingly radical 'demonization' that has essentially placed it beyond the pale of established politics in the UK. After Thatcher came to power in 1979 the British Labour Party underwent a generalized crisis, as more traditional socialists found themselves increasingly at odds with centrist liberals. This division could also be roughly, but imprecisely, cast in terms of an internal opposition between a 'hard left' and a 'soft left' (see Panitch and Leys, 2001: 167).

As this opposition heightened while Labour was out of office in the 1980s, it spawned a 'Militant Tendency' that rose to prominence in leftist city councils such as the one in Liverpool (see Panitch and Leys, 2001: 214ff.). The backdrop to these developments was widespread, union-led opposition to Thatcher's policies of deindustrialization and privatization. This came to a dramatic head with the miners' strike of 1984–85, with harrowing scenes, broadcast across the nation, of picketing miners being beaten down by mounted police. This was the context of my teenage years and I remember vividly the apocalyptic sense of hopelessness that imbued the Thatcher years of the 1980s, particularly in the north of England.

Democratic politics is rarely anything like a high-minded debate conducted in unmediated face-to-face encounters. What was going on during the neoliberal transition in British politics was largely refracted through the distorting lens of the mass media, where portrayals of a 'loony left' takeover of the British Labour Party in the early 1980s abounded. The kind of political-cultural transformation Hoggart (2009) and Williams (1961) had argued for in the 1950s and 1960s requires a democratized communications infrastructure that would diversify the transmission of information and take it as close as possible to a local level of self-organization.

By contrast, the kind of transnational telecommunications monopolies that exist in the twenty-first century are as far away from Williams's vision as the Soviet state monopoly on communications would have been in his own day (see McChesney, 2015). The 'soft power' of the mega corporations that dominate the media and entertainment sectors is immense and, arguably, one of the most corrosive factors in contemporary liberal democracy. What we experience as individuals we can feel as a member of a class: being unable to control the way we are presented to others gives rise to an acute sense of vulnerability, instability and – eventually – profound resentment.

Jones puts the matter bluntly: 'From salt of the earth to scum of the earth. This is the legacy of Thatcherism – the demonization of everything associated with the working class' (2016: 72). This demonization was the ideological dimension of neoliberal economic policy which, rather than doing away with the state, refashioned state agency more and more in favour of corporate interests. While 1970s Britain was clearly something other than a social and political utopia, it did represent the most economically equal British society ever achieved (see Harvey, 2005: 17). Elements of this equality managed to survive into the 1990s. For example, attending university between 1990 and 1994 I was among the last generation in the UK to benefit from a university education free of tuition fees and supported by a state-funded maintenance grant. Under neoliberalism, by contrast, post-secondary education is presented as a matter of an individual's ability to calculate a balance between opportunity and risk vis-à-vis their own entrepreneurial potential as a 'free player' in the capitalist labour market. No one should expect, as the classic neoliberal argument goes (see Friedman, 2002: 85–107), to be publicly financed beyond basic education. But this logic plays out very differently according to the socio-economic position of the individual in question.

This is the well-known sleight of hand whereby 'equality of outcome' is reduced to 'equality of opportunity'. As Jones writes: 'Politicians, particularly in the Labour Party, once spoke of improving the conditions of working-class people. But today's consensus is all about *escaping* the working class. The speeches of politicians are peppered with promises to enlarge the middle class. "Aspiration" has been redefined to mean individual self-enrichment: to scramble up the social ladder and become middle class' (2016: 10). It is clearly not sufficient, however, to present the shift towards neoliberalism as simply something imposed on the British working class. While there was strenuous and sometimes dramatic popular opposition to this shift, Thatcherite policy also worked because it genuinely tapped into established working-class habits of mind. As Hoggart's (2009) analysis recounts, British working-class communities were prone to resent any sense of dependency on institutionalized assistance. Getting by using only one's own means and efforts was generally seen as a marker of social respectability.

But this ethic of self-sufficiency did not rule out an equally important sense of group solidarity. This latter element was most apparent in the institution of the trade unions, where mutual aid sprang from the lived experience of an individual worker's weakness in the face of an employer's superior bargaining power. Neoliberal ideology seizes on the ethic of self-reliance but removes the preconditions for what we might call collective autonomy. The closest it offers as a surrogate for this is the mirage of 'consumer power', knowing all along that the field of consumption is inevitably determined largely by the producer, distributer and retailer rather than by the highly diffused and uncoordinated actions of consumers.

The political genius of neoliberal ideology lies in its ability to turn members of the working class against each other, thereby largely distracting attention from the minority who prosper under such conditions. With New Labour abandoning or taking for granted its core voters, the British working class was essential left without party-political representation. As explored in our first chapter, centrism in liberal democracies tends to produce widespread political disaffection which, in turn, gives rise to the xenophobia and racist scapegoating that typically act as the affective vehicle of populist politics. Without the prospect of having an effective voice within the established party-political system, working-class politics can then easily rise and fall with the vicissitudes of particular populist demagogues.

An 'outside' or 'other' of working-class collective identity can be constructed in various, largely incoherent ways. As we saw in the case of the study of Boston workers conducted in the early 1970s by Sennett and Cobb (1972), such racism and xenophobia are a *reaction* within, not somehow an essential attribute of working-class culture. Abandoned to a political wilderness, the British working class is reduced to constructing a negative social identity: I may be working class, but at least I am 'genuinely' English, and so forth. In the immediate aftermath of the Second World War, it was this very logic of social compensation through scapegoating that Jean-Paul Sartre (1995 [1948]) so effectively diagnosed and exposed in his excoriating critique of European anti-Semitism. For our purposes here, it is necessary to underscore the point that such intolerance is not intrinsically endemic to working-class culture, but rather a symptom of a neoliberal condition where working-class interests are severely marginalized and working-class identity is constructed as a badge of dishonour.

Work and social value

The underlying purpose of the current analysis is to construct a deeper, more historically grounded interpretation of contemporary populism than the one generally presented. While it would be foolish to ignore the features of xenophobia, racism and nativism, my argument here is that these aspects do not get to the heart of contemporary populism. Focusing exclusively or predominantly on these characteristics will not, I contend, allow us to understand populism adequately.

As was set out in Chapter 1, the democratic project in all its guises makes a fundamental appeal to the popular will. In a democracy, whatever particular mechanisms are put in place must be seen to make good on its claim to be rule by the demos. Under the neoliberal conjuncture it is not so much that the appeal to the popular will is flatly denied or repressed completely. Instead, it is recast in the image of individualized entrepreneurialism. As neoliberal economic policy refashioned the role of the state it shifted the onus of responsibility for employment from the state to the individual worker. Under neoliberal governance, state agency is fixed in advance on elevating the interests of the 0.1 per cent of wealth owners over everyone else, making any pretence to genuinely egalitarian social justice empty sophistry on the part of the political class. The Great Recession that began in 2008 made clear, however, the unevenness and hypocrisies of this position: while millions of workers lost their jobs and their homes, the banks, deemed 'too big to fail', were bailed out in the UK, US and elsewhere (see Harvey, 2010: 1–12).

The harsh ethics of responsibility meted out to workers under neoliberalism highly stigmatizes those considered to be failing to make the most of their 'opportunities'. In the workplace, this often translates into an abusive one-way relationship, where workers are expected to do everything within their power to enhance their productivity but the employer is under no obligation to safeguard jobs or work conditions. Under industrial capitalism worker productivity measured by output relative to labour hours quickly established itself as the primary yoke placed around the workers' necks. But, as Marx saw clearly by the 1860s (Marx, 2010), this masked the primary economic function of the capitalist mode of production, namely the creation of 'surplus value': the value added by workers above and beyond what they receive back in remuneration.

The conceit of neoliberal ideology is that workers get back what their work is essentially worth. The concept of surplus value makes clear, to the contrary, that such an equation between work and wages can never be arrived at under capitalism in principle. The key question, when related to contemporary liberal democracies, is how much surplus value production is invested in social rather than private goods. The present state of the most neoliberalized societies, such as the US and UK, is clearly characterized by an alarming bloat of private wealth at the expense of public goods and institutions. The social body at large is being remorselessly neglected and deprived, while a narrow demographic band of the ultra-rich continues to surfeit on excess profits.

In terms of lived experience, neoliberalism and its attendant economic inequality is felt in different ways. The precariousness of work for most workers under neoliberal conditions is ideologically transformed into something seemingly positive. The very idea of hankering after stable employment, with recognized seniority, pay scales and a guaranteed works pension, is seen as anachronistic and at odds with the dynamism of the 'gig economy'. Long before entry into the workplace, working-class young people are admonished to develop transferable skills, constantly seek new training and educational opportunities, be willing to move to where the jobs are, and so forth. In the UK, much attention has been paid recently to the phenomenon of 'zero hours contracts', where a worker has no guarantee of any level of minimum employment within a given time frame (Syal and

Stewart, 2018). Unpaid internships, long established as the norm among young workers in the UK and the US, have also received high-level political attention. What these developments all point towards is the increasing disposability of the worker. How, under such conditions, can the working class generate a sense of value in and through work?

The generalized crisis of value generated in and through work is the preoccupation of Richard Sennett's more recent research. In the previous chapter, we considered the investigation of Sennett and Cobb (1972) into the experiences and attitudes of the Boston working class. Already then, long before the Reagan era of the 1980s, workers were found to be plagued with doubts and anxieties concerning their social status. The early phases of a profound shift from manufacturing to service sector jobs and the 'knowledge economy' was revealed to be deeply troubling to many middle-aged male workers. A profound ambivalence was setting in, whereby the needs of a younger generation to break out of older patterns of work were validated, but the prospect of the new kinds of work was seen as devaluing for older workers.

Three decades on from this seminal study, Sennett has increasingly focused on the notion of craft as an antidote of sorts to the neoliberal devaluation of work. He captures the tension in the following manner:

> The more one understands how to do something well, the more one cares about it. Institutions based on short-term transactions and constantly shifting tasks, however, do not breed that depth. Indeed the organization can fear it; the management code word here is ingrown. Someone who digs deep into an activity just to get it right can seem to others ingrown in the sense of fixated on that one thing – and obsession is indeed necessary for the craftsman. (Sennett, 2006: 105)

While neoliberal work management prizes mobility and adaptability, craft calls for careful diligence to one thing; while the entrepreneurial imperative insists on moving quickly from one opportunity to the next, always with an eye on future possibilities, the craft-worker remains rooted in the present task at hand. As Sennett puts it in another of his works:

> Craftsmanship names an enduring, basic human impulse, the desire to do a job well for its own sake. Craftsmanship cuts a far wider swath than skilled manual labor; it serves the computer programmer, the doctor, and the artist; parenting improves when it is practiced as a skilled craft, as does citizenship. In all these domains, craftsmanship focuses on objective standards, on the thing in itself. (Sennett, 2008: 9)

In other words, seeing work as craft involves recognizing good work as an end in itself. Because craft-based work is guided by settled standards, it ideally lessens the self-doubt and status anxiety that typically plague the neoliberal worker. But Sennett is not naive here; he does not advocate a nostalgic return to craft-based production in ignorance of the prevailing norms of neoliberalism. Instead, craft is offered as a counter-practice or model of resistance that has the potential to restore social recognition to the worker and to the working class.

The key characteristic of craft-based work, on Sennett's analysis, is its being predicated on social recognition. Both the attainment and the execution of a craft is subject to evaluation by others who possess and know that craft. In other words, the very existence of craft-work attests to socially recognized value, goods in common. Equally, Sennett insists that the capacity for craft is widely dispersed throughout human society and ultimately grounded in our innate predisposition for cooperative activity. Just as young children learn or devise rules of a game and then test each other's ability to practise the game in accordance with the rules, so too craft-work relies on successful social communication.

By contrast, the schema of work-value under neoliberalism is individualistic and meritocratic. While at first glance measuring the value of a person's work through merit seems eminently benign and fair, Sennett points out that there is a subtle but invidious shift involved relative to any craft-based valuation. One way to capture the difference between craft- and merit-based work is to recognize the key role played by the notion of potential in the meritocratic paradigm:

> Within the meritocratic scheme there is thus a soft center in evaluating talent; that soft center concerns talent conceived in a particular form, as potential ability. In work terms, a person's human 'potential' consists in how capable he or she is in moving from problem to problem, subject to subject. The ability to move around in this way resembles the work of consultants, writ large. But potential ability cuts a larger cultural swath; it is a damaging measure of talent. (Sennett, 2006: 115)

As opposed to craft, which is something painstakingly acquired and becomes a semi-permanent possession of the worker, 'potential' is a somewhat numinous quality that can only ever be pointed to but never positively demonstrated. Sennett sees the ideology of potential at work from the beginning of a child's life, when institutions of schooling are geared up to identify it from the earliest stages of formal learning.

Drawing on the work of Foucault (1995), Sennett is acutely aware of the tendency within neoliberal culture to subject individuals to a constant regime of testing. Of course, performance of a craft is also subject to testing, but the way knowledge and competence are typically tested today in contexts of formal learning is quite different to the kind of peer-to-peer recognition and critique involving in practising a craft. One need only think of the ubiquitous 'standardized testing' within schooling. Such tests, theoretically designed to eliminate bias in evaluation, are generally experienced by students as deeply alienating and disciplinary in nature (see Ravitch, 2014). At worst, they often seem irrelevant to the possession of the very knowledge supposedly being tested. Similarly, contemporary workers are increasingly subject to productivity evaluation that diminishes rather than enhances any sense of satisfaction or pride in one's work. In line with Foucault's well-known analysis of Jeremy Bentham's model prison (Foucault, 1995), the neoliberal regime of testing gives rise to the generalized apprehension of being under constant disciplinary surveillance.

Cooperation and creativity

The purpose of the current chapter is to explore the nature of contemporary work in order to understand more adequately how and why the current condition of the working class might give rise to the populist sentiment. One standard account given for contemporary populism is resentment towards the political class and perceived elites more generally (Mudde, 2004: 543). In the case of the Brexit vote, such an explanatory framework holds that a majority of the electorate felt alienated from the 'establishment' and seized an opportunity to thwart its desire to maintain the status quo. But cynicism towards politicians has been a constant in modern democratic history, and so we need a more specific diagnosis to make sense of the current populist sentiment.

One measure of adequacy here would be historical breadth, and that is why, in Chapter 3, I retraced some aspects of the historical formation of a self-conscious working-class in nineteenth-century England. In the current chapter a more restricted long view is offered, one that takes in the period, beginning in the early 1980s, during which liberal democracies have been subject to neoliberalization. Neoliberalism is a complex political paradigm, but it is, in my view, best seen in terms of a reaction against the rise of the working class as a dominant political force. Seen in this light, the essentially negative task of neoliberalism is to reverse all the gains made by the working class between the mid-nineteenth and mid-twentieth centuries in terms of direct and indirect political power, share of wealth and income, and cultural capital. One crucial way in which neoliberalism has undermined the social standing of the working class is by simultaneously strengthening the moral imperative to be in work while radically undermining the freedom of the worker and the intrinsic value of work itself.

In ideological terms, as Harvey notes, neoliberalism hinges on the idea that 'human well-being can best be advanced by liberating individual entrepreneurial freedoms and skills within an institutional framework characterized by strong private property rights, free markets, and free trade' (2005: 2). The concern for individual liberty is not, of course, something original to late twentieth-century neoliberalism, but was already a key issue for classic nineteenth-century liberals such as John Stuart Mill (1989 [1859]). In very broad terms, it is fair to say that opposition between liberal individualism and socialist collectivism was *the* key ideological fault line in nineteenth-century politics. With the advent of neoliberalism in the twentieth century, socialism is seen through the lens of communist totalitarianism, so that ideological opposition to 'big government' and an overweening state apparatus becomes a key concern. Accordingly, we see this concern assume centrality in the works of key neoliberal thinkers such as Friedrich Hayek (2007 [1944], 2011 [1960]) and Milton Friedman (2002 [1962]).

One of the core appeals of nineteenth-century socialist thinking was for a shift from the competitive imperative naturalized by the defenders of capitalism to the mutualism, solidarity and cooperation between members of the working class. It is imperative to note, however, that this basic concern of socialism was never simply a matter of theory alone but also, crucially, a matter of workers' concrete collective praxis. In the latter respect, it was the myriad social institutions embodying the socialist perspective – trades unions, night schools, cooperative associations and so forth – that should be regarded as the pre-eminent achievement of working-class political praxis.

Socialism stands for a way of organizing social relations that accentuates mutualism and collaboration. In terms of human well-being, the fundamental question is whether such working together is an essential element of human flourishing. The liberal tradition that stems from such thinkers as Mill (1989) regards society and government largely as limiting factors on individual development. Through this lens, the political imperative relates to limiting interference – by broader society and government – of the individual's right to pursue whatever life is deemed best as long as it does not infringe on the ability of others to do the same (Mill's famous 'harm principle'). As we have seen, fear of the working-class masses (especially in the context of political agitation and demonstration) played a large part in giving rise to a liberal social philosophy preoccupied with defending the development of the individual largely unfettered by the demands of society as a whole. Arguably, what neoliberal ideology does is ally this defence of individualism with an unconditional faith in the benign consequences of a largely unregulated 'free market'.

The pressures placed on the individual to achieve social mobility based on their own meritorious actions is the leitmotif of Sennett and Cobb's (1972) original study of the Boston working class. Building on the findings of this study, Sennett's more recent analysis places the emphasis on the spectre of meaninglessness that haunts the contemporary neoliberal workplace. Part of what contributes to the experienced valuelessness of contemporary work, he argues, is that our inherent capacity for cooperation is being more and more repressed and denied expression within the neoliberal labour market:

> We are losing the skills of cooperation needed to make a complex society work. My argument is not grounded in nostalgia for that magical past in which things seemed inevitably better. Rather, the capacity to cooperate in complex ways is rooted in the earliest stages of human development; these capacities do not disappear in adult life. These developmental resources risk being wasted by modern society. (Sennett, 2012: 8–9)

One of the great changes wrought by the deindustrialization process in liberal democracies such as the US and UK from the 1960s on was a shift from large workforces, often organized by labour unions, to the smaller, more fragmented workforces typical of the service sector. Office of National Statistics figures show a steady growth in service sector employment and a commensurate drop in manufacturing employment from around 1966 (Chiripanhura and Wolf, 2019). Such fragmentation of the workplace has lessened both the potential for and efficacy of union organization. Casualization of employment also followed, whereby the precarious pact arrived at between large employers and employees which involved a degree of mutual commitment was shattered. The consequence of this is that work, on the side of both the worker and the employer, is increasingly seen as a temporary arrangement of convenience.

While workers' expectation of stable employment diminished, the state's commitment to support those out of work became more and more conditional on testing a person's willingness to work. The notion of 'workfare', pioneered in the US and since implemented in various guises in the UK and other European countries, constitutes an important shift in the sense of care the state has towards unemployed workers (Handler, 2003; Rothman, 2016). Under neoliberalism, there has been an inexorable change in social responsibility, away from a state that is duty bound to provide adequate care for all citizens towards a model where everyone should be prepared to take whatever work is made available to them, regardless of suitability or any sense of workplace dignity. This change goes hand in hand within the intensified focus on individualized entrepreneurialism.

Sennett's (2008) celebration of craft-based work is in part supported and in part contested by McRobbie's (2016) analysis of the iconic role played by the 'creative class' in the context of neoliberalized work. Like Jones (2016), McRobbie emphasizes the watershed period in British politics marked by the accession to power of New Labour under Tony Blair in 1997. While Blair inherited rather than inaugurated neoliberal governance in the UK, his decade of rule made manifest the separation of the modern British Labour Party from its roots in socialism and the working-class struggles of the nineteenth and twentieth centuries. In many ways, the New Labour project saw Labour return to a kind of progressive laissez-faire liberalism typical of nineteenth-century British politics: committed to 'opportunity for all' but at ease with seeing the free market as the natural context in which maximized opportunity and fairness of outcome could be achieved. Above all, for both organizational and rhetorical purposes, New Labour was intent on lessening the formal ties that connected the party to the trade union movement (Panitch and Leys, 2001: 253–4). This break was driven by ideological motivations but was made materially possible by the fact that, through the 1980s and 1990s, the Labour Party was funded proportionately less by union contributions and more by money from wealthy donors (p. 236).

McRobbie's (2016) focus with respect to the transformation wrought by the New Labour project is on the construction and consolidation of what might be called a new social imaginary for the realities of work. Trade unionism arose historically through the recognition that conditions of work could only be improved and safeguarded if workers banded together through the mechanism of collective bargaining. Neoliberal governance, by contrast, seeks to dismantle trade union power in order to 'liberate' individuals from such collectivism, setting them free to pursue their own ways and means of working. Along the way, McRobbie argues, New Labour sought to replace the socialist understanding of work with a neoliberal conception of creativity:

> Work is not there, because in this rhetorical world it is business and entrepreneurship that now count, and so ideas of working life or labour process do not figure, since these ideas are too sociological; they are explicit reminders of what is now being superseded by an entirely different mode of activity, one that is nebulous, self-directed, taking shape with less 'interference' by the state, and not in any way connected to an industrial policy. (2016: 61)

The keyword in this shift is entrepreneurship. As Foucault (2008) deftly diagnosed in his lecture series from 1978/79, the social paradigm of neoliberal thinking involves each person becoming an entrepreneur of themselves. In this context, any boundaries between work and life, production and consumption become blurred: my life is a kind of perpetual self-improvement project and the purpose of my consumption is to produce my own satisfaction. The idealized neoliberal subject is someone who is constantly 'working' on themselves, striving to maximize their potential for self-satisfaction (Dardot and Laval, 2014: 330–1). As Foucault (2008) notes, this perspective leaves no room for the key socialist idea of alienation in and through work: work, in neoliberal terms, is not a set of conditions imposed on the worker from the outside, but instead explained as an inner drive and ability to choose superior conditions of flourishing (McNay, 2009: 65).

The matrix of choice in which the neoliberal worker finds themselves is one that always favours dynamic risk-taking over stability and predictability of employment. Under neoliberal governance the worker is left, in both positive and negative terms, to themselves. With the neoliberal state distancing itself from any paternalistic care for the welfare of its citizens, workers are now called upon to celebrate this very condition of precariousness. As McRobbie notes:

> Neoliberalism succeeds in its mission in this respect if a now very swollen youthful middle class bypasses mainstream employment with its trade unions and its tranches of welfare and protection in favour of the challenge and excitement of being a creative entrepreneur. Concomitantly, when in a post-industrial society there are fewer jobs offering permanent and secure employment, such a risk-taking stance becomes a necessity rather than a choice. (2016: 11)

McRobbie's analysis stems in large part from her experience as an academic who supervises graduate students striving to become successful young 'creatives'. Inheriting the cultural studies perspective pioneered by Hoggart and Williams, McRobbie is well placed to appreciate how her own place of work – the university – has been subject to relentless neoliberalization in the past few decades. Just as early British cultural studies interrogated the supposed British meritocracy of the late 1950s and early 1960s, so McRobbie seeks to deconstruct the oppressive ideology of personal talent and entrepreneurial self-advancement disseminated by contemporary neoliberalism. And just as German critical theory in the 1940s drew attention to the development of a 'culture industry' (Horkheimer and Adorno, 1997), so McRobbie maps out the realities of a contemporary creativity industry:

> Indeed, I argue that the word 'creativity' displaced and supplants the word 'culture', since it is less contaminated by the Marxist legacy that in the space of British public debate at least still lingers round the edges of many such debates. Creativity becomes something inherent in personhood (childhood, adolescence and young adulthood; less often, old age), which has the potential to be turned into a set of capacities. The resulting assemblage of 'talent' can subsequently be unrolled in the labour market or 'talent-led economy'. (2016: 10–11)

Just as Williams (1958) famously argued that 'culture is ordinary', neoliberalized work is founded on the rhetorical conceit that creativity is ordinary. But whereas Williams focused on culture in the sense of intricate networks of social connection in everyday working-class life, the neoliberal rhetoric of creativity is predicated on the supposed inevitability of competitive individualism. The neoliberal perspective generates an extremely quixotic social imaginary: all have the capacity to 'make it', though few will; everybody gets what they deserve, though nothing as such (beyond Adam Smith's 'invisible hand') ensures that this will be the case. In McRobbie's study, we encounter many graduate students who are already holding down multiple casual jobs and who can only look forward to making a further precarious living, struggling all the time to find remunerative outlets for their creative abilities and credentials.

One of the key shifts brought about through neoliberalism is that creativity begins to stand for something not evidenced within but rather opposed to labour. Under New Labour, McRobbie argues: 'Creativity was disconnected from any idea of labour, even as it was being promulgated as a source for growth and wealth creation. At the same time the anomalous nature of this kind of work … also constitutes a challenge for organized labour itself' (2016: 69). McRobbie's critique of the 'creative economy', most forcefully championed in the UK by New Labour in the late 1990s, does not take issue with the increased economic resources and accessibility brought about by Labour policy at that time. It is rather a question of New Labour having undermined the social and political functions of cultural production in favour of an image of creativity tethered to individualized success:

> But if the policy language of the new creative economy had not been cast in such deeply individualistic terms and had instead been concerned with questions of how artists and creative people could work in ways that would be valuable to others, and with how they could engage in pressing social and urban issues, the current self-conscious hipness and the distance from the normal life of the working-class or migrant city would not have been so acute. (McRobbie, 2016: 157)

McRobbie directly reacts to Sennett's (2008) celebration of craft as a means of restoring the dignity of contemporary work. While she recognizes some genuinely emancipatory potential in Sennett's position, she largely sees his perspective as vitiated by socially conservative and patriarchal residues. This criticism seems to me fair insofar as a mere appeal to craft will do nothing to interrupt the constantly accelerating circuits of skill and product obsolescence characteristic of the neoliberal capitalist economy. Sennett's perspective also appears to be largely anti-statist, appealing more to the precursors of industrial labour unions, the craft guilds, as a context of work organization. The strength of Sennett's analysis, on the other hand, is that it attempts to restore real, experiential content to work, rather than accepting the traditional Marxist premise that work will always be, under capitalist conditions, inherently alienating and oppressive.

Solidarity and resentment

Despite the differences, it is important to underscore the key common ground between Sennett and McRobbie, namely their shared recognition that what is lost to the working class under neoliberalism is any coherent and nurturing sense of mutuality and social recognition. When critiquing the plight of workers under neoliberal governance, it is important to avoid romanticizing earlier periods as some sort of halcyon day of the working class in Britain or elsewhere. Just as Hoggart (2009) made clear that British working-class life was steeped in resentment towards perceived outsiders, Sennett (2012) looks back on how the same working-class sentiment was evident in the Boston working-class subjects of his original 1972 study:

> It would be quite wrong to imagine working-class cohesion made for happy citizens. Outside the workplace, the workers I interviewed in Boston felt slighted by the elite liberals who made policy for the city, and they transformed these slights, as in a distorting mirror, into negative attitudes about poor African-Americans below them; Boston workers were all too vehement in expressing ressentiment. The social bond occurred more narrowly inside the workplace. (2012: 150)

Clearly, then, it would be a mistake to view the working-class solidarity in evidence prior to the neoliberal shift in the US or UK as constituting some sort of ideal condition of generalized social solidarity. While a certain tranche of workers did enjoy superior work conditions and relative job security, this was achieved at a time when women and racial minorities were largely excluded from such jobs. The trade unions themselves, so instrumental in securing better workplace conditions, were slow to adopt the causes of racial and gender equality and acted to protect their core workers at the expense of others (Hill, 1996; Lawrence, 2016). As was also noted when considering Hoggart's (2009) account, traditional British working-class life involved a rigorous sense of self-sufficiency in addition to the willingness to lend a hand when others were in need. The internal divisions within the class were also assiduously maintained: there was a strong sense of who was or was not 'respectable' within a working-class community or neighbourhood.

With these caveats in mind, it is nevertheless widely observed that neoliberalization has brought with it an ethos of alienating individualism that has acted to dissolve the social bonds of working-class life. Much of this dissolution has to do with concrete economic changes in the life experience of workers. While many skilled British workers in the 1960s and 1970s could rely on a job that would pay enough to support a household, that rewarded seniority and was union protected, in the majority of cases now working-class jobs are radically insecure and short-lived and provide only a subsistence wage. When working brings with it the experience of survival rather than flourishing, there is little room for cooperation and solidarity with one's fellow workers. The upshot of this survival economics, for Sennett, is that any sense of underlying common purpose within the workplace is lost:

> By progressive I mean here that a good polity is one in which all citizens believe they are bound together in a common project. Social capitalism created that common project through civic institutions based on a military model; the vice of social capitalism was the iron cage of solidarity. The new institutional order eschews responsibility, labeling its own indifference as freedom for individuals or groups on the periphery; the vice of the politics derived from the new capitalism is indifference. (2008: 164)

As Sennett and Cobb (1972) observed decades ago, working-class Americans reserved their most virulent criticism for those fellow members of their class who appeared to live a life of ease on state welfare. In Britain, this trope of the benefits scrounger is a staple of the right-leaning tabloid press. As Jones (2016) remarks: 'It is true that bashing "welfare scroungers" may be more likely to attract the support of a low-paid worker than a millionaire. After all, if you work hard for a pittance, why wouldn't you resent the idea of people living a life of luxury at your expense?' (2016: 91). The political message endlessly rammed home is: look, this is what happens when you construct a welfare system – those who truly deserve are taken advantage of by the lazy and feckless. The ultimate effect of this media portrayal is to stigmatize any receipt of benefits as ethically indefensible state dependency.

At present, as we will examine in more detail in the next chapter, the idea of a universal basic income (UBI) has captured the imagination of many thinkers and politicians of the left (and even some of the right). But this idea is unlikely to be translated into a national programme in a country like the UK any time soon, due to the general opprobrium that attaches to welfare dependency. One of the many paradoxes of the neoliberal order is that it strengthens the imperative to work just as it undermines the average benefits and attractiveness of working. 'I must work; I cannot work' becomes the contradictory mantra of the oppressed working class under neoliberal governance.

Some years ago, I published a book called *Constructing Community* (Elliott, 2010). Part of that project involved analysing the ambivalence towards the notion of urban community among social theorists. In a long line of social research going back to pioneering figures such as the sociologist Georg Simmel in his 1903 essay 'The Metropolis and Mental Life' (1971), the city is found to separate individuals, making them retreat into an isolated interiority in the face of too much sensory stimulation and a sense of others as an oppressive omnipresence in the urban environment. In opposition to this thesis of mutual indifference, there is another trend within urban theory celebrating the lively mixture and interactivity of the urban context (see Jacobs, 1989 [1961). But even those who celebrate the urban experience, such as Iris Marion Young (2010, 2011), warn that we should resist the temptation to want to render urban community too cohesive and homogeneous. Sennett (2017), in *The Fall of Public Man* (originally published in 1977), is one of the first urban theorists of this tendency to caution against looking for too much consistency and commonality in the urban community.

There is a further strand to this debate worth bringing up in the present context. This is the well-attested fear of the urban crowd as a display of working-class democratic power. The most recent salient case is that of the 2011 Occupy movement. This was a novel form of political praxis, distinct from the more traditional modes of appearing in public space, such as the demonstration. It also directly showcased the issues of austerity politics and challenged metropolitan governments' toleration of having members of the public take control of public space. As such, it was an important test of substantive as opposed to purely formal and procedural democracy. As urban historians and theorists have been pointing out for decades (Smith, 1996; Graham, 2010), neoliberal urban policy has led to the privatization of much ostensibly public space, more draconian policing of public demonstrations and protests, as well as acute gentrification. While there was some sympathy at the outset for the Occupy movement, popular media moved quickly to point out the hypocrisy or pointlessness of allowing the massed public to remain assembled on the street for any length of time (see Kaminer, 2011; Rawstorne, 2011).

While there have been many well-informed and cogent defences of the Occupy movement (see Graeber, 2013), it arguably constituted an act of collective desperation that was never likely to bring about long-term political or social change. Looking back at the social history of the workers' movement in Britain, it can be seen that instances such as Chartism were the result of long-established networks of solidarity with relatively clear political demands such as universal suffrage. While it was styled on the events in Cairo during the Arab Spring, Occupy Wall Street lacked the clarity of purpose evident in Egypt. Certainly, there was a sense that all the ills of neoliberalism identified in this book were to be contested. But it remained unclear how the acts of occupation were to become an effective mode of political praxis to this end.

If Sennett's contention is correct, then a generations-long ascendency of neoliberalism in places like the US and UK has fatally undermined the habits of cooperation, making the very preconditions for progressive collective action questionable. He notes:

> Solidarity has been the Left's traditional response to the evils of capitalism. Cooperation in itself has not figured much as a strategy for resistance. Though the emphasis is in one way realistic, it has also sapped the strength of the Left ... The new capitalism permits power to detach itself from authority, the elite living in global detachment from responsibilities to others on the ground, especially during times of economic crisis. Under these conditions, as ordinary people are driven back on themselves, it's no wonder they crave solidarity of some sort – which the destructive solidarity of us-against-them is tailor-made to provide. (Sennett, 2012: 279)

Sennett's contrast of cooperation and solidarity is intriguing. His argument offers a potential way forward for a progressive restructuring of work that would combat the social harm done by neoliberalization. The distinction is directly relevant to the analysis of populism developed in this book, in light of the fact that traditional leftist politics is predicated on the construction of a working-class identity. It could be readily argued that this was the direct result of the dominance achieved by Marxist thought, which insists on the construction of proletariat class consciousness as the essential precondition for progressive social change. The relative deindustrialization of the world's leading economies arguably removed the economic conditions for such a mode of socialist politics. In the world of fragmented workforces, such as the post-2008 financial services sector studied by Sennett in *Together* (2012), the class-based politics of work could find no purchase. Lower-level managers who found themselves out of work as the financial crisis hit had few resources for experiencing solidarity following the sudden loss of their employment and social status.

As he readily acknowledges, Sennett's vision of an alternative to neoliberal capitalism follows another nineteenth-century model of socialism to the one offered by Marx and Engels. This alternative vision chiefly expressed itself in the Arts and Crafts movement, advocated for by John Ruskin from the 1850s on and put into more practical effect by William Morris in the decades that followed. While Marx and Engels saw industrial work as a necessary evil and looked to a future where the burden of work was minimized through intensified automation and fairer distribution, Ruskin and Morris campaigned for the restoration of intrinsically rewarding craft-based production.

In the Marxian heritage we can see already a certain post-work hypothesis, whereas Sennett, in line with Ruskin and Morris, seeks to restore value from within the practice of work itself. Sennett's position is lent support by a distinct trend in contemporary neoliberal societies towards localized, craft-based production. Disaffection with homogenized global production has led to many locally produced alternatives: microbreweries, coffee roasters, clothes manufacturing and so forth. Many contemporary urban theorists (Heying, 2010; Marotta and Heying, 2018) have drawn attention to this craft-work renaissance that has flowered across cities in the US, UK and elsewhere over the last decade. This development gives rise to the following question: what is the renewed tendency towards local, craft-based production responding to and what might it foreshadow as a possible future of work?

The future of the working class

Throughout this book I have advanced the general argument that the roots of contemporary populism reside within the neoliberal shift that has occurred over the last four decades. It follows from this that the only way to correctly respond to populism is to address this neoliberalization. The specific argument presented in this chapter is that any credible political opposition to neoliberalism must begin with the issue of work and pursue a concrete programme of radical reform within the realm of work. This necessary focus on work is the primary reason why it is premature to give up on the political project of working-class emancipation.

We began this chapter with a consideration of Jones's (2016) observations on the demonization of the British working class. Jones's argument, in a nutshell, is that the working class in the UK has been left without effective party-political representation since the formation of New Labour in the mid-1990s. This has allowed a centrist consensus to emerge according to which the only legitimate social aspiration is a desire to escape the working class. I believe this analysis is largely correct but underplays the degree to which there are elements in the Thatcherite, and later Blairite, worldview that were and remain intrinsically attractive to the British working class. It is inadequate to see the British working class as lacking in agency and merely as a victim of a neoliberal political programme that sought to marginalize and devalue working-class identity.

Harking back to our first chapter, we can bring back into play at this point Mouffe's (2000, 2005) idea that the drift towards political centrism among the established major liberal democratic parties has alienated a large swathe of voters by establishing the justified belief that 'they're all the same, so what's the point of voting for them?'. Political apathy or a search for new, anti-establishment parties or politicians are two reactions to this realization. In the case of the EU membership referendum, the mantra of the Brexit campaign was the blunt but seductive slogan 'Take back control'. What was meant, how the change was to happen, and from whom control would be taken back were left largely undetermined. In the immediate aftermath of the referendum it quickly became clear that the in/out binary posed by the referendum masked a bewilderingly complex political reality. Presumably, any honest representation of Britain's membership of the EU at the time would have cast the question in nuanced relational terms, but political rhetoric broadcast through mass media is rarely so sophisticated.

Effectively representing working-class concerns has been a problem throughout modern British political history. The great attraction of a referendum is that it gives the impression that the popular will be readily translated into an immediate political decision. While anti-immigrant sentiment is often cited as a core concern among those who wished the UK to leave the European Union, it is clear that no major British party is prepared to oppose immigration into the country in general terms. If, as it is also commonly argued, Brexit voters wanted to see a return to more robust national sovereignty, then they must still contend with the political mediations of the British parliamentary system.

It is extremely questionable, in my view, whether the UK outside of the EU will be any more democratically accountable to the electorate than it has been within the EU. As the process of devolution in Britain in recent decades attests, there is every prospect that the process of further regional autonomy or semi-independence will continue once the Brexit process is formally completed. However things play out post-Brexit, it seems unlikely that Britain's future outside the EU will do much in and of itself to address the challenges faced by the working class under neoliberal capitalism. In fact, given the business-friendly attitude of the governing Conservative Party, there is every chance that British workers will enjoy less and not more workplace protections after the UK has completed its withdrawal from the EU (Morris, 2019).

For all the political pyrotechnics that were related to the Brexit process, the British political establishment and business as a whole have always wanted as little unpredictable disturbance of the status quo as possible. It is a salient feature of neoliberal governance more generally to desire to minimize 'politics' as undesirable background noise. While the famous neoliberal adage 'never let a good crisis go to waste' holds true within strict limits, a predictable baseline of political reality is generally a precondition for neoliberal business-centric governance. Given this, there is significant scope for widespread disappointment and further backlash among the Brexit-voting working class once it becomes unmistakeably obvious that their material conditions are no better and perhaps significantly worse.

Of course, nobody could have foreseen that the UK's transitional period following its formal withdrawal from the EU in January 2020 would take place during a global pandemic. It is widely predicted that the UK and US are likely to experience levels of unemployment unknown since the protracted recession of the 1980s or even Great Depression of the 1930s (see Inman, 2020; Mutikani, 2020). The fate of the working class is tied, as ever, to the fate of work. Under current conditions, with the US and UK national governments allocating billions to keep people in work during the worst of the pandemic, a stark choice appears to be looming: either to reform the work sector, allowing for such mechanisms as job share and elements of UBI to become permanent, or to allow an exacerbated condition of under- and non-employment to became a permanent condition for an increasing proportion of the working class.

For my part, I do not believe the former is a genuine option under neoliberal governance, as it would involve levels of permanent state intervention in the labour market to which such governance is opposed as a matter of principle. Consequently, the only politically progressive option is to begin the long task of turning back the tide of neoliberalism in earnest and across the board. As work becomes less rewarding and more a source of stress rather than satisfaction, workers will seek ways to justify their working life instrumentally. If work demeans rather than elevates social prestige, workers will look for ways to find that prestige elsewhere or identify outlets for their resentment. Debt-financed consumerism offers many palliatives to the injuries and hardships inflicted by neoliberalized work. It provides a mirage of plenty and luxury to mask the poverty and depravations suffered by workers; it constitutes a currency of social recognition in a condition where any sense of workplace community has all but disappeared. But a debt-financed consumer-driven economy has its limits, as we are currently experiencing: our consumer behaviour runs up against the imperative to safeguard human life. In reality, of course, under neoliberal capitalism human life and well-being are constantly traded off against profit in all sectors of the economy.

A key tenet of neoliberalism, according to David Harvey, is that 'social good will be maximized by maximizing the reach and frequency of market transactions, and [neoliberalism] seeks to bring all human action into the domain of the market' (2005: 3). But the principal feature of any tradable commodity is its fungibility, that is, its ability to be exchanged for other goods. Take parents' capacity to care for their children. In Britain's neoliberal economy, many households require two incomes to stay afloat. But childcare, especially for very young children, is also expensive. In this situation, childcare becomes fungible in such a way that the loss of earnings for parents will be weighed against the cost of paying for professional childcare. However, the more profound question raised is whether it is socially desirable that something as intrinsically valuable as rearing a child should be reduced to a commoditized market transaction.

The main concern of the socialist project is to prevent this process of reification in relation to core human values. Work, considered simply, is simply purposive human action generating social value. Neoliberalism constructs work as an issue of individual satisfaction but displaces or eclipses the question of shared value. As with the libertarianism with which it is allied, neoliberalism presents work as a question of an individual's inalienable right to sell their own labour in an untrammelled marketplace. But the market is not, in and of itself, a democratic forum where all negotiate with equal power and prestige. Historically, it was the recognition that those who control capital also largely control the conditions of individual workers that sparked the kinds of resistance, organization and mutual aid analysed in Chapter 2. The challenges of contemporary work are, of course, very different two hundred years after the start of the workers' movement in Britain. But some of the principles remain the same. Progressive politics in contemporary Britain can only make good on the true spirit of democracy and equality by overturning neoliberal governance – by reconstituting the political power of the working class.

5

The politics of work

Work and social value

In the first three chapters of this book I set out and defended a theory of democracy that centres on the principle of popular sovereignty; grounded that principle in the concrete history of working-class struggle; and further interpreted democracy in line with Raymond Williams's idea of the 'long revolution'. Along the way, it has been repeatedly stressed that democratic culture is essentially about sharing decision-making power over the material conditions of everyday life as widely and deeply as possible. In Williams's own words: 'General participation in common decisions can be argued on grounds of principle. It is, after all, the deepest principle of democracy itself' (1983: 102). In the last chapter, the basic argument was that the last four decades of neoliberal governance in places such as the UK have entailed a radical rollback of the democratic gains made in the preceding two centuries. It was further argued that changes in work over the same period have been accompanied by an ideological devaluation and erasure of working-class values.

When socialist thinking and praxis developed in the nineteenth century, it was predicated on a profound experience that the freedoms made possible by the capitalist economy were essentially 'bourgeois' and, in material terms, limited to the propertied rather than the working class. This experience also entailed a profound ambivalence with respect to industrial work: was the ultimate point of any kind of socialist transition to abolish or redistribute work? Was it primarily about the spoils of industrial production and so a redistributive question, or had it more to do with the social or 'spiritual' values associated with industrialization? In the latter case, the underlying value that tended to occupy centre stage was that of freedom understood in terms of self-determination. In a word, was generalized freedom a condition compatible with industrial capitalism or did it intrinsically entail that the majority toil under conditions that approximated to forced labour? One early response to this question, famously castigated by Marx and Engels in their 1848 *Communist Manifesto* (2004), was the 'utopian socialism' represented by the likes of the Welsh industrialist Robert Owen. At New Lanark in Scotland, Owen managed a pioneering experiment in a workers' industrial cooperative at the outset of the nineteenth century (Siméon, 2017).

It was to such historical cases of worker self-organization that the classical liberal thinker John Stuart Mill (1989) turned in his posthumously published *Chapters on Socialism*, arguing that much social good might be achieved by promoting experiments in worker-managed production. As a senior employee of the East India Company for most of his adulthood, Mill had no principled misgivings about industrial capitalism and world trade dominated by imperial politics. Indeed, earlier in his life, in 1848, he had authored his *Principles of Political Economy* (Mill, 2008), which became – and remained – the standard book on economic theory in British universities long after his death in 1873. Mill's championing of worker self-organization followed from his progressive politics that included the promotion of universal public education. If formal education was an essential precondition for creating an informed public to allow an extension of the franchise, then educated citizens must also be encouraged to take on roles of responsibility in all important domains of shared social existence, including in the workplace.

These connections between work and shared decision-making have, I contend, been severed under neoliberal governance in very specific ways – principally, as we saw in the previous chapter, by rhetorically transforming work from a collective activity generating social value into a matter of the self-promotion of the individualized entrepreneur. The truly grotesque levels of wealth and income inequality realized under contemporary neoliberalism are, in large part, justified by an ideologically driven representation of corporations led by putatively visionary and truly exceptional CEOs. Corporate managers, at the highest levels, are presented as maverick geniuses operating in an exclusive sphere that the regular worker can scarcely hope to enter.

In this process we can see an insidious parallel between the adulation of dynamic high-level executives and the social currency of personalities in the entertainment sector. Recurring to Hoggart's presentation, in 1957, of traditional working-class values (2009), we recall that an earlier attitude of suspicion and cynicism towards the ruling class has been gradually transformed into one of passive acceptance and even adulation in the face of manufactured celebrity. Of course, familiar celebrities are often presented as 'just one of us' who happen to find themselves in the limelight. Thus, there is a curious symbiosis between the cult of celebrity manufactured by the entertainment industry and the social currency of democratic politicians. The key point to be made about this parallel is that it places the people in the position of passive spectator rather than promoting an active citizenry making good on the democratic principle of self-rule.

But this is more than a mere parallel, as we increasingly see the way in which the line between 'serious' politics and 'light' entertainment becomes blurred. The political leaders in the US and UK at the time of writing (2020) – Donald Trump and Boris Johnson – both worked hard to establish a public profile in the entertainment sector before attaining high public office. Contemporary politics is more stage-managed than ever, nowhere more than in televised leadership debates where politicians and parties increasingly insist that any direct interactions with the voting public be either meticulously planned in advance or else completely avoided. This manner of media representation cannot but attach a certain aura to high-profile politicians on a par with celebrities, something which makes them feel both intimately familiar and yet far removed from the material reality of the electorate.

As Adorno (1994) claimed, there is a certain totalitarian colouring to the process of a celebrity morphing into a charismatic politician: such a politician presents themselves as a friend of the people, somehow more real that the 'ordinary' political class. At the same time, political presentation and debate gravitate increasingly towards personalities and away from the substance of policy. This culture of celebrity also enjoys an effective means of defence: when criticism does surface it is all too easily dismissed as nothing more than sour grapes by those who do not enjoy such success. The underlying political problem in all this is that the process of democratic representation is stunted and deadened as a consequence.

In Adorno's stark terms, in an essay from 1967, this intertwining of mass entertainment and democratic politics increasingly tends to offer up politicians to the public as perfectly fashioned desirable commodities: 'Cultural entities typical of the culture industry are no longer *also* commodities, they are commodities through and through' (Adorno, 2001: 100). Personality politicians represent a chasm between the action of the electorate and the political class. According to Hoggart's account (2009), this sense of distance was endemic to traditional British working-class culture. When this culture has been systematically devalued over four decades of neoliberal hegemony, however, the working-class reaction to the political class is prone to become highly volatile and even explosive. This would go some way to explaining the current wave of populism expressed in the Brexit referendum result in the UK and the election of Donald Trump in the US. As a result of highly mediatized presentation and the cult of the media personality, the reality principle in democratic politics can readily become eroded and attenuated for the electorate. Media presentation through such means as televised debates is often reduced to a crass assessment of how well a particular candidate managed to project their personality. Behind it all, the nagging doubt that democracy is really a game played by others well beyond our sphere of influence becomes hardened in the mind of the public.

Work, control and freedom

The cult of personality also opens up imaginary and consoling vistas beyond the everyday struggles of work. No doubt the working class has always dreamt of a world beyond or without work. As already noted, nineteenth-century socialism essentially offered two means of realizing this dream: on the one hand, reducing the burden of work through automation and fairer distribution; and transforming work into something intrinsically valuable to the worker and general society, on the other. In the first, Marxian approach lies the appeal to the progressive abolition of human labour. Thanks to capitalist pressure to increase profit by developing labour-saving technologies that decrease the costs of labour relative to the value of output, a socialist future beyond work was inadvertently made possible through advances in mechanization.

For this possibility to become a reality, however, it would be necessary to bring about a profound shift in the social order such that workers seized control, in Marx's terms, of the 'means of production'. A question that haunted this version of socialism was: what were people to do after the revolution? If work had been largely abolished through rationalization and collectivized ownership of the means of production, then a person's meaningful activities would have to take place outside of productive work. The only existing model for this, however, was the bourgeois culture that had arisen on the foundations of the capitalist economy. Hannah Arendt (2018) saw here the fatal flaw in Marx's political thinking: his desire to liberate workers from work would simply end in the banality of mindless consumption, such as Arendt already saw in evidence in 1950s America.

What, then, of the second version of socialism which, in opposition to Marx, looked to make work intrinsically rewarding for all? Early in the nineteenth century, as mentioned, there were experiments in 'utopian socialism' such as the worker cooperative of Robert Own in New Lanark. In the latter half of the same century and inspired by the cultural thinking of John Ruskin, William Morris offered a vision of craft-based work with certain nostalgic overtones in favour of a pre-industrial economy. Richard Sennett's sociological analysis and case of a contemporary revival of craft-based work in many ways represents a continuation of the tradition of utopian liberal socialism.

But Sennett's line of thinking remains vulnerable to Marx's claim that the capitalist mode of production is not amenable to a quiet revolution of crafters working in virtual seclusion and ultimately dependent on the relatively deep pockets of a consumer with more discretionary income than most. While it is easy enough to agree with Sennett's claims that a renewed appreciation of craft would do much to overcome the alienation faced by the average neoliberal worker, he offers us little sense of the means to achieve such a shift at any large scale. Islands of craft production will always exist where there is a sufficient client base with spending power to purchase such goods. Given the general tendency of the neoliberal economy to produce patterns of starkly uneven distribution, however, most will place price before quality in order to meet their day-to-day material needs.

While the political visions of Marx and Morris each have their problems, it is a common underlying principle that interests me here: *worker-controlled production*. While wealthy liberal democracies now boast better educated populations than at any previous period, the average worker has seldom been so powerless in the workplace. This is profoundly puzzling. Certainly, had Mill been around to witness it, he would no doubt be aghast at the abject servitude and impotence of the working class who live in the richest countries today. The relative lack of worker protections, the precarious tenure of position and, above all, the prevailing passivity of most workers would have shocked him as signs of gross illiberality.

Conditions of work such as prevail in twenty-first-century Britain and America cannot possibly be seen as consonant with anything like collective freedom. With echoes of Mill's positive social vision of generalized individual self-development, Erich Fromm in 1942 presents us with a stark alternative between a free and an unfree political order: 'Democracy is a system that creates the economic, political, and cultural conditions for the full development of the individual. Fascism is a system that, regardless under which name, makes the individual subordinate to extraneous purposes and weakens the development of genuine individuality' (Fromm, 2001: 236). Fromm also insists that the realization of free social conditions requires the spontaneous activity of the individual 'not only in certain private and spiritual matters, but above all in the activity fundamental to every man's existence, his work' (2001: 234). As I argued in a previous book on the politics of climate change (Elliott, 2016), neoliberal governance tends to frame all issues of social value in terms of survival economics. This reflects back on the domain of work, thereby providing the ideological justification for maintaining subsistence wages for the working class no matter what levels of wealth and income prevail more generally. This tendency is deeply ideological and, indeed, quite remarkable given the startling levels of surplus production realized under neoliberal capitalism. The same projection of scarcity is evident in all domains. As a consequence, the neoliberal political order is essentially at odds with substantive democracy – thereby amounting to 'fascism' in Fromm's terms – due to the fact that its projection of crisis economics will always regard popular control of economic activity as a luxury we are unable to afford. In a word: a constantly manufactured state of emergency within the neoliberal order necessarily renders genuinely participatory democracy an impossibility. If genuine democracy is ruled out in principle under neoliberalism, what routes remain open to us to revive democratic political culture? Following the general argument offered in this book, the basic answer to this question involves empowering the working class. In broad terms, the debate bequeathed by the socialist tradition turns on the question whether such empowerment should be realized within or beyond work. Hence, in this final chapter I discuss some aspects of the contemporary leftist debate concerning work. In particular, a line of argument has opened up recently which revives earlier notions of a post-work economy. Proponents of a progressive post-work society argue that it is the only viable option in the face of an ongoing wave of computerized automation. When even highly skilled professionals in education, law and healthcare are threatened with technological obsolescence, so the argument goes, the only credible progressive strategy is to introduce a universal basic income (UBI) that would guarantee a decent standard of living for all regardless of any socially useful work performed.

While proponents concede this sounds like a tough sell, they argue that it is the only way to counteract the deepening crisis of wealth inequality and precariousness. I am deeply sceptical of this argument, however, as it is at odds with a number of salient features of contemporary social-political reality. Chief among these is a lack of recognition of the manifestly autocratic nature of neoliberal governance. While the UBI proposal is indeed very attractive to progressives, there is little hope that it will gain any high-level political traction as things stand. Second, I do not believe that broad support could be found for a radical separation between social value and work across liberal democratic societies. While the identity and cohesion of the working class has been critically undermined over the last forty years, the value of work as an individualized moral imperative has been dramatically heightened. It follows from this, I believe, that any political party or platform that calls for a radical separation between work and social value will garner only minority support. The lesson to be drawn from the recent resurgence in craft-based production, I believe, is that it is not work per se that is seen as the problem but the kind of work generally available. Nevertheless, there is a growing chorus of leftist thinkers who believe the only way forward is to prepare for a world beyond work and thereby advocate mechanisms to sever the time-honoured connections between productive work and monetary and social value.

Neoliberalism and the roots of populism

In the 1980s, as the collapse of the Soviet Union loomed and neoliberal government became an established fact in the UK and US, the onetime inevitability of a transition to world socialism looked like an absurdity. Socialism no longer offered an image of a desirable future but instead of an intolerable and defunct past. Rather than the emancipation of workers and the realization of social justice, socialism now meant the tyranny of an all-embracing state bureaucracy and generalized material scarcity. But neoliberal governance, at least in liberal democracies such as the United Kingdom, never supplanted other political futures simply by being imposed from above. Instead, it needed to tap into traditional values already at play within working-class life for generations, the most important of which was the pride taken in hard work and self-sufficiency.

Thus, when Thatcher came to power in Britain in 1979, appeals to individual self-advancement through reforms such as the 'Right to Buy' scheme were very effective in winning over the British working class (see Murie, 2016). This policy allowed residents of council-owned properties to buy the place they lived in, at a price well below market rates. While this was undoubtedly profitable for many working-class households in the 1980s, it has had the overall effect of vastly reducing the stock of publicly owned housing. Ideologically, the policy is predicated on the belief that it is morally superior for individuals and families to own rather than rent the place they live in. Now, after four decades of exponential property price appreciation in the UK, one of the many contradictions of this neoliberal policy is that most working-class families and individuals are more or less obliged to rent as house prices on the open market are well beyond their means. Thus, what started out under Thatcher as a manifestation of individual autonomy – a way of escaping the reach of an overzealous state apparatus – has led to a collective condition of greater scarcity and precariousness.

Individual ownership of housing is complemented, in the neoliberal paradigm, by entrepreneurialism with regard to one's labour power. Marx's critique of capitalism rests on the proposition that class antagonism makes the generalized alienation and domination of the working class by the property-owning class inevitable. Neoliberal theory counters this perspective by asserting the libertarian axiom that the free market ensures the liberty of the individual to dispose of their labour as they wish. Dispossession occurs not when the capitalist market obliges the worker to sell her labour to the highest bidder, but rather when the state interferes with this market exchange through legislation and taxation (Nozick, 2013 [1974]).

The obvious problem with this libertarian proposition is that it ignores differentials of power in the bargaining position of the individual worker relative to employers. The traditional mechanism for redressing this imbalance is the labour union. Under neoliberalism since the early 1980s there has been a precipitous drop in union membership in both the UK and the US. Union membership is disproportionately present in both the public sector and in larger workplaces. According to the UK Office of National Statistics (ONS), the number of public sector employees shrank from 7 million in 1980 to 5.4 million in 2018. This compares with an increase from 18 to 27 million workers in the private sector over the same period (Chiripanhura and Wolf, 2019). As a statistical bulletin from the UK government from May 2019 states (UK Department for Business, Energy and Industrial Strategy, 2018: 6), in the four decades between 1978 and 2018 total union membership in the UK halved from 12 million to just over 6 million. The same report notes that the 'proportion of employees who belonged to a trade union in larger workplaces was 30.6% in 2018, compared to 15.2% of employees who are employed in a smaller workplace (less than 50 employees)' (p. 9). The most striking figure of all is that union membership in the public sector is four times greater than it is in the private sector (52.5 per cent as against 13.2 per cent respectively in 2018) (p. 12).

Accordingly, one of the most effective ways to reduce the economic and political influence of unions is to bring down levels of public employment. Once again, according to the neoliberal perspective this is not an injury done to workers but rather represents their emancipation into the free market of work. While some workers may find a liberalized economy more exhilarating and rewarding, the net effect, as we see all around us in mature neoliberalism, is collective insecurity. If the socialist dream of the nineteenth century centred on empowering workers in and beyond the workplace, the contemporary worker in neoliberal Britain has arguably never felt weaker or more demoralized. This is in part due, as we saw in the previous chapter, to the relentless denigration of working-class culture that has accompanied neoliberal governance in the media and entertainment sectors. The kind of self-supporting local networks of solidarity recorded by Hoggart have largely disappeared as advances in communications and media technology have isolated individuals ever more thoroughly within their homes. This isolation has also occurred, as noted by Sennett (2012), in the workplace, where workers feel little sense of mutual care and responsibility, either with regard to fellow workers or management. While they are far from perfect, unions offer an institutionalized context in which common worker concerns and grievances can be articulated and potentially resolved with management. In the absence of this institutionalized framework, workers are thrown back onto their own resources in a pitiless struggle for survival and advancement.

The decline of union membership and representation matters to our political culture because, as Sennett (2012) observes, it tends to corrode our inherent capacity for cooperation. If we work, for decades, at jobs which seem not to bind us but largely separate us from our fellow workers, then this spirit of antagonism is bound to affect, in profound ways, our sense of collective responsibility when we participate in democratic politics. Just as our managers fail to hear us, to treat us respectfully and humanely, so are we likely to transfer these negative experiences to our sense of those who manage our public affairs. That is, under such working conditions, dissatisfaction with our experience of work can be readily transposed to attitudes towards the political class. As I argue throughout this book, those who would dismiss populism as little more than intolerance and xenophobia are overlooking what has happened to liberal democratic political culture over four decades of neoliberal reform.

Our cultural milieu and social structures are formed at a much lower and more immediate level than that of institutionalized national politics. They are initially constituted in childhood within our immediate and extended family, before broadening in the context of formal education and then further overlaid by our experience in the workplace. All of these contexts are, arguably, seminal for and thus determining of political culture. Rather than emancipating us, neoliberalization has involved relentless imposition of economic austerity and coercion, resulting in a generalized experience of instability and powerlessness. If, as I am arguing in this book, the root cause of contemporary populism is this shared working-class experience of cultural denigration, workplace impotence and economic precarity, then the antidote can only be a radical overhaul of the present neoliberal dispensation. More specifically, we cannot hope to have a vibrant democratic political culture unless we truly democratize such social spheres as child-rearing, education and, most crucially, the workplace. Populism, therefore, should not be regarded, at base, as a mass working-class protest based on ignorance and racism. Instead, first and foremost, it should be seen as a reaction to a social and political order that has for decades undermined the conditions of action and existence among the working class.

André Gorz and post-work socialism

As noted numerous times in this book, I am acutely aware of the general reticence and scepticism regarding any attempt to reinstate the 'working class' as a key concept of political theory. In response to this reticence I have made clear that my allegiance here is to 'New Left' cultural theorists such as Raymond Williams. While Williams was certainly a champion of working-class struggle (he often recalls his father's experience of the General Strike in Britain in May 1926), he also makes clear his dissatisfaction with orthodox Marxian economism (see Williams, 2005: 35–55). Williams's cultural rather than economic characterization of class allows for a more nuanced, qualitative articulation of the concept. Above all, Williams – in common with Hoggart and the Thompsons – was committed to the task of promoting an ideal of democracy in terms of generalized self-representation and self-determination.

With the shift to the neoliberal order of the early 1980s, the generation of British intellectuals to which Williams belonged could hardly hope to represent the cutting edge of the political zeitgeist. The defence of working-class everyday culture could be easily dismissed, in a context of mass unemployment, as an embarrassing anachronism. Opening the gatefold sleeve of The Smiths' album *Hatful of Hollow* at the age of fifteen, I felt a natural affinity with the sentiment of Morrissey's words in 'Still Ill': 'And if you must go to work tomorrow, well if I were you I wouldn't bother.' If work was not to be had, the best compensatory attitude was surely to protest you didn't want to work anyway. The time was ripe for a form of socialism that rejected the orthodox Marxian centrality of the working class as the key locus of historical agency and of labour as the ultimate source of social value.

In work published from the early 1980s on, André Gorz argued that the concept of the working class that had remained central to socialist politics for a century and a half had run its course. Drawing on certain sentiments that had surfaced back in the May 1968 protests led by students and workers in the French capital ('Never work!' was one of the famous graffiti slogans of that time), Gorz argued that the successors to the socialist political project needed to accept that work should henceforth cease to be a critical concern. Instead, the challenge for a reorganized left would be establishing a progressive political programme where social value was definitively and irreversibly severed from productive work. In his own words: 'The ideology of work, which argues that "work is life" and demands that it be taken seriously and treated as a vocation, and the attendant utopia of a society ruled by the associated producers, play right into the hands of the employers, consolidate capitalist relations of production and domination, and legitimate the privileges of a work elite' (Gorz, 2012: 56). Gorz felt that socialism had to evolve beyond the cult of work. The dramatic rise in unemployment across liberal democracies in the early 1980s and the shadow of further automation and worker redundancy convinced him that the only progressive way forward was a managed decoupling of value and productive work. He argued this for ecological as well as for social-political reasons and his thinking still has great relevance to contemporary conditions. Indeed, as we shall see, he is an originator of the post-work paradigm currently gaining traction again within leftist thought.

Gorz begins his analysis by encapsulating Marx's original idea of worker emancipation: 'The transformation of work – of *all* work – into an autonomous activity was, according to Marx, the meaning of communism as a lived historical horizon' (Gorz, 2012: 56). Just as libertarianism appeals to *individual* autonomy in and through work, nineteenth-century socialists such as Marx appealed to *collective* autonomy in work. But Gorz believes that the process of Western deindustrialization he is living through in the 1980s calls time on this Marxian prospect. Henceforth, collective freedom must be gained outside of and beyond work: 'Now, there is no social space in which "true work" – which, depending upon the circumstances, I prefer to call "work-for-oneself" or "autonomous activity" – can deploy itself in such a way as to *produce society* and set its stamp upon it. *It is this space we have to create.* In this regard, a reduction in working hours is a necessary, but not a sufficient, condition' (Gorz, 2012: 57).

For Gorz, generalized freedom will henceforth have to be realized outside of the actually existing workplace. The argument here is not that work will simply disappear. Gorz recognizes that material transformation is an essential necessity for maintaining human existence. It is rather that the privilege granted to work – and hence the working class – as the fundamental source of social meaning and value must be abandoned. In terms of social policy, the intermediate goal should be to reduce work to the lowest possible level consistent with the maintenance of material well-being. As we will see in the next section of this chapter, when we consider the work of the contemporary technological accelerationists, some leftists feel that this reduction will take place of its own accord as technology advances.

But the mere reduction of total human labour will do nothing to bring about collective emancipation unless what Gorz (2012) calls the 'social space' for such freedom is created in the process. We can readily see how contemporary neoliberalism is emphatically *not* producing such a space. As human labour becomes redundant in an ever-increasing array of economic spheres, the tendency is to lower wages in such a way that people are forced to compete with automating technologies. The 'sharing economy' of such companies as Uber co-opts and thereby subverts the prospect of a post-work utopia by having people compete against each other in freelancing work that tends to undermine the material conditions of more traditional workers. In general, as Gorz would readily acknowledge, keeping people at work (or searching for work) for long hours fulfils the invaluable political function of sapping their energy for other, potentially more socially transformative activities.

The challenge of Gorz's analysis is not easily dismissed. He was convinced that leftists needed to bid farewell to the very idea that the socialist future amounted to the transfer of political power to the working class. The working class, he contended, was being liquidated by the very forces of production that had brought it into existence two centuries earlier. Crucial to this argument is Gorz's contention that the 'modern concept of "work" ... represents a sociohistorical category, not an anthropological one' (Gorz, 2012: 54). In other words, work should not be grasped as an essential feature of human society, but rather as a contingent aspect of capitalist industrialization. One obvious problem with this approach is that it appears to ignore the fact that the relative deindustrialization of the wealthier economies did not amount to global deindustrialization, but instead involved a process of offshoring labour to places where costs were lower, workers less protected and potentially more tractable. In Britain, it was clear that the destruction of the industrial base in the 1980s was, at least in part, motivated by a deliberate project of undermining the political power of the industrial working class and their influential unions. Furthermore, even if the prospect of a 'post-work' social condition became viable in the wealthier nations, what of the plight of workers in the industrializing developing world? One of the great strengths of the Marxist vision is that it appeals to 'workers of *the world*', rather than exclusively to this or that pocket of workers within the early industrializing economies.

There are further objections to Gorz's argument. One might seem purely semantic but is actually a matter of substance. Restricting the notion of work to the organization of production under globalizing capitalism (roughly the 1820s to the 1960s) appears arbitrary and leaves us with the problem of defining socially meaningful activity outside this time period. This objection is tied up with a further one. Gorz calls for a general abandonment of the connection between work and social prestige; in other words, he thinks any vestige of the work ethic should be driven out. But this is easier said than done. The dialectic of work and leisure (as non-work) is historically embedded in the formation of social class. Thorstein Veblen's *Theory of the Leisure Class* (2009), published in 1899, is the classic articulation of this phenomenon, whereby conspicuous signs of freedom from productive labour are socially encoded so as to gain esteem from peers.

This connection between freedom from labour and social esteem also played its part in the seminal period of the workers' movement in Britain (and elsewhere), which involved a crucial struggle to limit hours of the working day and week, the creation of a work-free weekend and so forth. As with Veblen's privileged 'leisure class', however, freedom from labour does not of itself generate social prestige. Rather, the time freed up needs to be spent in activities of leisure that signal to others one's condition of relative freedom. In the case of the British working class, this took the form of involvement with associations organized by and for workers, whose connections were forged, first and foremost, at a common workplace and through shared experiences of work. In other words, abandoning work as a source of social value leaves us arguably without means for the creation of alternative sources of such value. Finally, we recall the thesis of the 'culture industry' (Horkheimer and Adorno, 1997), which makes clear how advanced commodity capitalism offers up increasingly sophisticated simulacra of desirable lifestyles that alienate the working class from the realities of everyday life. While the premise of Gorz's argument – that workers in the neoliberalized economy find it progressively more difficult to identity with work – is valid, his conclusion that work should cease to be a crucial issue in progressive politics is false.

These objections, however, do not amount to a wholesale rejection of Gorz's line of thinking. It is undoubtedly the case that the working class of contemporary Britain has little in common with the working class of the 1830s or even the 1960s. The neoliberal workplace is severely fragmented due to the more transitory nature of the workforce, organizational restructuring and the sheer mobility of global capital. But these have also been salient features of the capitalist labour market throughout its history. Their relative novelty only emerges when viewed in contrast to the uncharacteristic stability of the post-Bretton Woods world economic conditions of the 1950s and 1960s. Thus, the idea that deindustrialization or intensified automation, in and of themselves, have predetermined impacts on the distribution and nature of work is false (Pitts *et al.*, 2017). In this, Gorz's thinking on work is dangerously close to a kind of leftist defeatism that unwittingly echoes the ideological position of neoliberal proponents who insist that 'there is no alternative' to technology-driven skill obsolescence, mass unemployment and so forth. The key difference is that Gorz presents the situation as a retreat from work by the workers themselves, rather than something purposely realized by neoliberal government in reaction to supposedly immutable economic realities of the 'free market'.

More strategically, and charitably, Gorz's position can be seen as part of a much-needed internal critique of leftist labour politics, in particular, of traditional labour unions. The history of the labour unions, as already noted numerous times, has tended to be quite reactionary in creating a dialectic of insiders, who deserve union protection, and outsiders, who do not. Sometimes the split has been between skilled and unskilled or semi-skilled workers; sometimes between nationals and non-nationals; men and woman; or whites versus non-whites. The ascension of so-called identity politics, particularly in the United States, has been instrumental in displacing or at least significantly qualifying class-based progressive politics. This was a necessary phase of reform within leftist politics but it has had the undesirable effect of splintering the progressive voice in organized politics. US media routinely refer to the 'African American vote', the 'Hispanic vote', and so forth, as though these were unproblematic social-political entities. In contemporary Britain, such blocs have been constructed in the media in starker terms, so that the Brexit vote is readily cast an act of revenge against the liberal political establishment by the 'white working class'. But the key point here is that the historical reality of the working class, in Britain and elsewhere, is complex and not simple. 'Working class', within a broadly Marxian and socialist understanding, refers to those who are, in varying ways and degrees, disempowered by the capitalist economic and social order. That covers a vast and varied multitude of those who, in one way or another, must sell their labour in order to live.

Recognizing this variety means that there is no difficulty in endorsing Gorz's sentiment when he writes: 'The new social movements will become the bearers of socialist transformation when they ally themselves not only with the "modern worker" but also with the contemporary equivalent of the disenfranchised, oppressed and immiserated proletariat – that is, with the post-industrial proletariat of the unemployed, occasionally employed, short-term or part-time workers' (Gorz, 2012: 73). The idea expressed here makes Gorz's work highly usable in our own times of advanced neoliberalism. In the present context, 'the workers' in a more pointed sense are those who lack work, both in suffering long-term unemployment and in being underemployed. Worklessness, which could be presented as a veritable progressive utopia in a period of full employment such as 1960s France, has created a capitalist dystopia in the twenty-first century.

While I recognize the salience of many elements in Gorz's attack on the traditional notion of the working class, I believe his advocacy for a transition to a post-work condition is neither realistic nor, ultimately, desirable. On the one hand, in direct opposition to Gorz's prognostications, the ideological dimension of the neoliberal transition brought with it a notable reassertion of the work ethic and an accompanying stigmatization of worklessness as a mark of individual failure. On the other hand, Gorz's formula for a post-work social condition is too vague to permit a credible foundation for a concrete programme of social reform: 'We have to start out from what work *is* and what it really means today in order to transform it, reduce it and expand the scope for autonomous activities, production for one's own use, and self-realization of everyone' (Gorz, 2012: 64). Again, what is not accounted for in this vision of a desirable post-work future is the capacity of shared workplaces to forge habits of cooperation and sentiments of solidarity. Unwittingly, Gorz's goal of 'self-realization for everyone' anticipates the contemporary social condition of neoliberalism, regulated as it is by an implacable imperative of individualized self-improvement.

Help yourself!

While his advocacy of a post-work condition may be untenable, Gorz's (2012) appeal to worker autonomy remains highly relevant in the context of the contemporary neoliberal work world. Studies on satisfaction or 'subjective well-being' at the workplace highlight the role of worker autonomy both with regard to work schedule and control over tasks done at work. As one such study reports: 'A number of forms of autonomy – job tasks, pace of work, manner of work, and informal flexibility – are found to have statistically significant positive impacts on reported satisfaction levels' (Wheatley, 2017: 321). The same study notes the reluctance managers have to grant further autonomy to those who work under them, 'as their primary role remains one of control and effort extraction' (p. 321).

While social science research has amassed an impressive body of evidence that highlights the positive impacts of worker control over their conditions of work, corporations have tended to address the symptoms rather than causes of worker dissatisfaction. Increasingly, the preferred corporate fix to the absenteeism and mental ill-health that often result from worker dissatisfaction is access to 'wellness' programmes. The underlying message of these programmes has a clear neoliberal provenance and proclaims: if you can't change your job, change how you think about your job. The traditional collectivist politics of labour is thereby replaced by an ethics of individualized self-improvement.

In their book *The Wellness Syndrome*, Cederström and Spicer (2015) offer an incisive critique of this contemporary corporate ideology. In the context of the contemporary work world, they argue, 'wellness' has become a moral imperative: 'While we often see it spelled out in advertisements and life-style magazines, this command is also transmitted more insidiously, so that we don't know whether it is imparted from the outside or spontaneously arises within ourselves. This is what we call the wellness command' (Cederström and Spicer, 2015: 5–6). While the common conditions of the working class are eroded under neoliberalism, individual workers are exhorted, with ever greater insistence, to maximize their capacity for well-being. While the palliative and narcotic effects of what Cederström and Spicer (2015) refer to as the 'wellness command' are not hard to recognize, counteracting its effects is another matter altogether.

One of the virtues Hoggart (2009) observed within the British working class was a relative lack of interest in individual betterment. Indeed, there was a tendency to distrust and pillory the ambitious working-class individual for 'getting above themselves'. Growing up in a northern English working-class culture, I recall feeling strong resentment towards those around me for a perceived lack of intellectual curiosity about what lay beyond their immediate everyday context. In fact, my wish to go to university was motivated in part to get away from what I then experienced as an indefensible parochialism. Breaking away from your community can be personally exhilarating but tends to produce bitterness among those who remain. As Hoggart observed several generations earlier than my own, a working-class community may offer a certain dependability to its loyal constituents, but it tends towards suspicion and hostility with regard to those who seek to move above and beyond it.

The fact that the neoliberal workplace is being colonized by wellness programmes and initiatives is a clear sign that nothing like Gorz's post-work society is in preparation. The notion being sold to workers here is that their employers are demonstrating care for the well-being of employees by offering resources that will help them maintain an optimum condition both within and beyond the workplace. There is no question that many companies and executives may be quite genuine in their concerns for workers' well-being. But it is not difficult to recognize that these developments are ultimately disabling rather than empowering workers in the workplace. Indeed, the underlying concern of corporations here is not worker health per se, but rather the negative impact on productivity, and ultimately profits, caused by worker absenteeism.

Beyond the autonomy level of individual workers, there are systemic economic factors that would appear to impact well-being within the working class. As William Davies (2015: 251) notes: 'Among wealthy nations, the rate of mental illness correlates very closely to the level of economic inequality across society as a whole, with the United States at the top. The nature and availability of work plays a crucial role in influencing mental well-being, as do organizational structures and managerial practices.' As Davies (2015) sees it, removing the institutionalized forms of collective action – principally, a union's collective bargaining power over workers' pay and work conditions – and the accompanying tendency to place all responsibility for work performance on the individual worker has led to a proliferation of mental illness among workers. According to a statistical report by the UK government's Health and Safety Executive (HSE) in 2019:

> In 2018/19 stress, depression or anxiety accounted for 44% of all work-related ill health cases and 54% of all working days lost due to ill health. Stress, depression or anxiety is more prevalent in public service industries, such as education; health and social care; and public administration and

> defence. By occupation, professional occupations that are common across public service industries (such as healthcare workers; teaching professionals and public service professionals) show higher levels of stress as compared to all jobs. (HSE, 2019: 3)

There are clear structural causes at work here: austerity economics which primarily affects public sector workers having to do more with severely constrained budgets; involuntary redeployment to different positions and locations; and inadequately supportive management. Neoliberal political thinking always draws on the libertarian belief in the supremacy of individual responsibility in order to downplay or contest these structural factors in worker satisfaction and mental illness. Just as neoliberals are committed to the fiction of market fairness and efficiency with respect to the allocation of goods and services, so too do they cling to the notion that individuals flourish the more they are left to themselves. But the complex fabric of capitalist society belies this naive faith in the supremely free individual. The opposing cardinal belief of socialism is that improvements in individual well-being are only ultimately desirable when accompanied by an overall advance in collective well-being.

Davies (2015) offers a detailed intellectual history of the neoliberal doctrine of individual well-being. In the present day, he notes, the cutting edge of this line of thinking is represented by a curious but powerful fusion of positive psychology, New Age self-help, and neuroscience. In terms of the dominant political narrative, this fusion amounts to a putative therapy for the social pathologies induced by advanced neoliberalism. The attraction of this therapeutic approach is that it promises to give back to workers the key thing they lack under neoliberalized conditions of labour: a sense of personal control. The difficulty for neoliberal governance here – evident since the earliest days of industrialized capitalism – is keeping workers in such a condition that they can continue to work productively but still be denied any material power over the productive process. In other words, the wellness agenda is neoliberalism's attempt to address the undesirable social symptoms of deregulated labour without dealing with their root causes. In Davies's words: 'The causes of mental health problems are obviously complex and do not lie simply in the economy any more than they do in brain chemistry. But it is the way in which these problems manifest themselves in the workplace, threatening productivity as they do so, that has placed them amongst the greatest problems confronting capitalism today' (Davies, 2015: 107). In a similar vein, Cederström and Spicer (2015) note the rapid growth, emanating from management theories and gurus in the United States, of a positive psychology trend calling on workers to manifest success through a relentlessly positive mental attitude. Like Davies (2015), these authors see the neoliberal workplace as increasingly dominated by a self-monitoring imperative that obliges workers to measure their level of success relative to their peers. It amounts to a kind of gamification of work, viewed positively by employers but tending to produce acute unhappiness among workers. We can see here, once again, a manifestation of what Sennett (2008) sees as the undermining of workers' skill acquisition. Craft, for Sennett, is a settled capacity of the worker to do something well and good work is a measure unto itself. Wellness indicators, by contrast, are numerical measures external to both the worker and to work. According to external metrics, relative improvement at work is always possible; indeed, peak performance is in a sense never attained as one can always go on to record a higher personal best.

In political terms, what the 'wellness syndrome' produces is a stark binary opposition between winners and losers within the neoliberal economy. What is presented as a motivational philosophy to realize one's highest potential to those in certain areas of gainful employment translates into punitive social policy for the 'losers'. Accordingly, the unemployed, already subject to social stigma for not contributing productively to the national economy, are to be further chastened within the welfare system for not trying hard enough. Neoliberal governance accordingly generates the following mantra: we know being in work is the best option for all; but you may not realize that yet, so we will make it very uncomfortable for you to be out of work. This political position became very apparent in 1990s America with the introduction of Clinton's Workfare programmes. As Cederström and Spicer put it: 'What is at stake here is a more thoroughgoing reframing of the question of governance. Happiness is not a cheap compensation for the weakened welfare state. Rather it is seen as a powerful attitude that can help people to change their situation. According to this logic, cutting benefits would not be a punishment but a necessary way to make people active' (2015: 78).

The neoliberal logic of work is thus characterized by this twin movement: as the traditional social rewards of work (primarily earning a decent living wage) fall away, the social and political imperative to be in work becomes more forceful. This is not so much a Marxian 'contradiction' as a lived tension of the neoliberal worker. It is also not exclusively a matter of fair remuneration, though this is part of the problem. The lack of fairness is readily interpreted, by the working class, as a sign that the 'ruling class' simply doesn't care about their conditions of existence. This perceived lack of care can also be understood as a lack of political recognition. Although the rhetoric of the neoliberal political class is peppered with empathetic allusions to the everyday struggles faced by the working class (clichés of 'putting food on the table', and so forth), it is hard to take these seriously when the speaker has little if any first-hand experience of hardship.

The positive psychology paradigm that is predominant in the rhetoric of corporate management is brought together with a New Age philosophy that both promotes a positive sense of self-improvement and yet makes individual agency something puzzling or even paradoxical. This stems from the fact that this approach holds, simultaneously, to the idea that positive change comes from within the individual practitioner through reflective mindfulness and to the notion that genuine satisfaction is a rare attainment, involving elements of good fortune or luck. This balancing act is necessary for the simple reason that neoliberal ideology rationalizes an actual situation where few win and many lose:

> Herein lies the paradox of the happiness command. On the one hand, we are asked to change our attitudes and to employ our willpower. When we focus our attention on the positive aspects of life, good things will come our way. Happiness, here, is an individual choice, available to anyone who is open to change his or her attitude. On the other hand, we are told that we cannot fool ourselves and just pretend to be happy. Happiness is a deep emotion which does not come easily, at least not the real kind of happiness. To achieve authentic happiness is not for everyone. (Cederström and Spicer, 2015: 70)

The doctrine of individual choice and responsibility is a mainstay of neoliberal thinking. It is manifest most obviously within the fiction of consumer choice. While this perspective is most obviously applied to individual commodity purchasing, it can just as readily be applied to educational provision (by those who call for the marketizing of education at all levels) or even personal relationships (encouraging a return-on-investment approach to any outlay of emotional labour). Aside from the naive rationalism at work in this approach to social structures and values, it presumes a perfect transparency of information that neoliberal economies fall far short of.

According to Davies (2015), the growth of the happiness industry is the long-term consequence of a dramatic shift in socio-economic thought that began with the unorthodox economic thinking of William Stanley Jevons in the last third of the nineteenth century. The groundwork for this shift had been established, Davies argues, by the success of Bentham's utilitarianism. This holds that all social good or 'utility' is to be gauged by the measure of individual pleasure over pain. In this framework, what counts as work loses all intrinsic value and becomes, in effect, a necessary evil as a means to attaining individual satisfaction: 'From this perspective, work is simply a form of "negative utility", the opposite of happiness, which is only endured so as to gain more money to spend on pleasurable experiences. Subjective sensation, and its interaction with markets, was elevated to a central question of economics' (Davies, 2015: 55).

This crucial change in economic understanding offers another way to account for Sennett's (2006) observations on the gradual reduction of workplace satisfaction. The new economic perspective, startlingly, assures us that work has no positive utility in itself. The problem with this, however, is that it leaves workers with no choice but to instrumentalize their work, thereby seeing it exclusively as a means to an end. It would appear, then, that the upshot of trends in social-economic thought as well as actual changes in the nature of work under neoliberal capitalism have converged on one and the same result: the hollowing out of the value of work. It follows from this that a common solution to the travails of labour can be achieved by moving to an economic condition that eliminates or at least minimizes human labour. Contemporary technologies of production would appear to make this idea of an economy beyond work a genuine possibility. An important strand of leftist thinking has arisen to articulate this goal and render it highly desirable. I would like to end this final chapter by considering, and ultimately rejecting, the arguments of those who offer a progressive politics beyond work.

Political futures and the end of work

Could the new socialist future be centred on the construction of a world without work? Should leftist thought carry to its logical conclusion the scepticism about the traditional centrality of working-class culture and consciousness and focus instead on the generalized obsolescence of human labour through computerized automation and artificial intelligence? Just as Gorz advocated in the early 1980s, a current strand of leftist thinking calls not for the defence of workers and jobs in the face of the technologically driven redundancy of labour, but rather for the intentional acceleration of this very process as the key to progressive politics today. The ascent of neoliberalism in the 1980s, we recall, coincided with a global economic crisis whose most salient feature was mass unemployment in the leading industrialized economies. The fights with organized labour that marked the foundational years of neoliberalization in the UK and US led to the demoralization of workers and an enforced and grudging acceptance of greater workplace precarity.

The successful effort made by neoliberal government to marginalize the power of unions placed capital firmly on the front foot in its relationship to labour. Workers' struggle continued, but henceforth that fight would be largely an individual rather than collective matter. Perhaps the best way to renew leftist, progressive politics is to maintain, as Gorz did four decades ago, that the traditional focus on the working class is untenable and accept that a future of mass worklessness is something to plan for rather than continuing to fight against it. Perhaps the time has in fact come to admit that capitalism has already created the possibility of a world without work and to acknowledge that the basic task now should be to accelerate rather than resist, mitigate or slow down the social-economic consequences of technological automation.

This proposition is skilfully and persuasively argued in two recent books: *Postcapitalism* by Paul Mason (2015) and *Inventing the Future* by Nick Srnicek and Alex Williams (2016). Mason, a British economics journalist, when advancing the case for technological accelerationism, praises André Gorz for arguing that work should cease to be the key concern of socialist politics, but rejects his assertion that the very idea of the working class should be abandoned. In fact, Mason's account depicts neoliberalism along similar lines to that offered by Harvey (2005), namely as a protracted and deliberate attempt to destroy the political power of the working class: 'Neoliberalism's guiding principle is not free markets, nor fiscal discipline, nor privatization and offshoring – not even globalization. All these things were by-products or weapons of its main endeavour: to remove organized labour from the equation' (Mason, 2015: 92).

Drawing on the thought of the Soviet economist Nikolai Kondratieff, Mason sees the rise of neoliberalism following the global recession beginning in 1973 in the context of long-term economic waves, typically lasting half a century. Beginning with the early Industrial Revolution in the 1780s, Mason identifies five such waves of global economic development. But the fourth wave that began with the Bretton Woods settlement following the Second World War has been disrupted and artificially prolonged, Mason claims, by three key factors: 'the defeat and moral surrender of organized labour, the rise of information technology and the discovery that once an unchallenged superpower exists, it can create money out of nothing for a long time' (Mason, 2015: 78). Drawing on his first-hand experience of the protest movements that arose in the wake of the 2008 Great Recession, Mason holds that working-class politics has undergone a paradigm shift. A key aspect of this change is that work and the workplace have lost their pivotal significance to political struggle. Accordingly, Mason argues that the working class has morphed into something quite distinct from the shape it has traditionally taken in socialist thought and praxis: 'Though it is not dead, the working class is living through a moment of sublation. It will survive in a form so different that it will probably feel like something else. As a historical subject, it is being replaced by a diverse, global population whose battlefield is all aspects of society – not just work – and whose lifestyle is not about solidarity but impermanence' (Mason, 2015: 179–80).

Mason's multi-layered analysis and extensive longitudinal economic data are interpreted through the lens of his conviction that capitalism is passing away. Mason is aware, of course, that the idea of capitalism's inevitable obsolescence can be readily seen as the Achilles heel of socialist thought. Nineteenth-century socialism was filled with a millenarian spirit presaging doom for the capitalist system. And yet capitalism, most lately in its neoliberal iteration, has survived all its death notices and gone from strength to strength since the 1940s.

Our focus in this book has not been on capitalism as such but rather on the conditions of democracy under neoliberal governance and how this may account for the current wave of populism. While neoliberal ideologues generally assert that capitalism in economics is the precondition for democracy in the political sphere, contemporary neoliberal capitalism, as we have seen, provides ample scope for questioning this article of faith. There is a widespread understanding that powerful global corporations and their democratically unaccountable CEOs have an immense and decisive influence over political decision-making in liberal democracies. From social issues such as health and education to the environment and welfare, the heavy hand of corporate lobbying is evident everywhere.

Well aware of this, Mason nevertheless repeats the time-honoured socialist mantra that the capitalists are unwittingly digging their own graves. The ongoing wave of computerized automation, particularly since the advent of widespread access to the Internet, has allowed corporations to make whole tranches of employees redundant. Some of those made redundant have found employment elsewhere, but the driving force behind this trend is to lessen the cost of labour to production. This development is complemented by another salient trend under neoliberalism, namely financialization. Mason provides some data to capture this process that pairs wage reduction with a shift from manufacturing to finance:

> The real wages of production workers in the USA have, according to the government, stagnated since 1973. Over the same period, the amount of debt in the US economy has doubled, to 300 per cent of GDP. Meanwhile, the share of US GDP produced by finance, insurance and real-estate industries has risen from 15 to 24 per cent – making it bigger than manufacturing and close to the size of the service sector. (Mason, 2015: 17)

The immediate effect of stagnating wages is hardship for workers and their families. But in a consumption-based economy it produces the structural tension that workers must continue to consume regardless of the spending power granted by work.

The 'solution' to this tension has brought about unprecedented levels of personal debt in the US and UK. Total US household debt (including mortgage debt) stood at $14 trillion by the end of 2019, double what it was a decade and a half earlier. Student debts alone account for $1.5 trillion of that total (Reuters, 2019). According to its latest report, the ONS calculated total household debt in the UK to stand at £1.3 trillion by March 2018, of which 91 per cent was property debt. Similar to the US, student loans are the main area of non-mortgage personal debt on the rise, increasing £7 billion between April 2014 and March 2018 (Office for National Statistics, 2019). For Mason, while automation has precipitated this debt crisis it also possesses the potential to usher in a progressive post-capitalist world. Given the exponential growth in information technology, what comes into view for him, as it did for Gorz, is a definitive separation of work and value: 'Info-tech makes the abolition of work possible. All that prevents it is the social structure we know as capitalism' (Mason, 2015: 181).

Srnicek and Williams's *Inventing the Future* (2016) offers a very similar argument to that proposed by Mason, though in a theoretical rather than economic mode of analysis. In common with Mason, Srnicek and Williams are seeking to conceptualize a renewal of leftist politics, particularly in Britain. Rhetorically, they wish to recuperate an earlier sense of socialism as a political programme for the future and so undo the neoliberal presentation of it as an antiquated remnant of earlier political struggles. Like Mason, Srnicek and Williams (2016) advocate an accelerationist programme with respect to automation and information technology, calling on the left to abandon its traditional preoccupation with job protection and creation: 'the tendencies towards automation and the replacement of human labour should be enthusiastically accelerated and targeted as a political project of the left' (p. 109). Most crucially, the post-capitalist condition will require the abolition of work:

> A twenty-first century left must seek to combat the centrality of work to contemporary life. In the end, our choice is between glorifying work and the working class or abolishing both. The former position finds its expression in the folk-political tendency to place value on work, concrete labour and craftwork. Yet the latter is the only true postcapitalist position. Work must be refused and reduced, building our synthetic freedom in the process. (Srnicek and Williams, 2016: 126)

It is important to note here that, unlike Mason, Srnicek and Williams follow Gorz in calling for the end of both work and the working class. If the systematic eradication of work is not done in the name of working-class emancipation, this is because the freedom to be gained beyond work relates to a plethora of social identities too broad to be subsumed under the idea of the working class. This rejection of class-based politics rests on a radical critique of what Srnicek and Williams refer to as 'folk politics', something they see in terms of a tendency in progressive thought and praxis towards small-scale community and peer-to-peer exchanges. Its most obvious manifestation is in environmental action, where it is evident in efforts to promote local or regional food chains and stewardship efforts. Within the socialist heritage there have been many attempts to sketch the superior virtues of small-scale and local organizations, not least in William Morris's vision of a renewal of pre-industrial craft guilds. For Srnicek and Williams, however, folk politics amounts to 'a set of strategic assumptions that threatens to debilitate the left, rendering it unable to scale up, create lasting change or expand beyond particular interests' (2016: 9). Folk politics is well illustrated, the authors feel, by the Occupy movement of 2011:

> Occupy constrained itself by enforcing a rigidly prefigurative politics. The basic prefigurative gesture is to embody the future world immediately – to change our ways of relating to each other in order to live the postcapitalist future in the present. The role of occupations is a classic example of this: they often self-consciously aim to enact the space of a non-capitalist world through mutual aid, rejections of hierarchy and rigorous direct democracy. (Srnicek and Williams, 2016: 34)

This criticism by Srnicek and Williams of 'prefigurative politics' relates to a notion developed by Raymond Williams (1989), namely 'militant particularism'. I have evaluated this idea positively in two previous books (Elliott, 2010, 2016). Williams, looking back on experiences of political struggle and social solidarity in the south Wales of his youth, was acutely aware of the capacity an attachment to place could have to anchor working-class struggle. But this 'particularism' of local struggle stands in tension with the universalism of Marx's conception of proletarian revolutionary praxis. In a Hegelian spirit, Marx conceived of the history of capitalism in global, world-historical terms. Accordingly, the envisaged transition to communism had to occur at the global, rather than national or regional, scale. The prospect of simultaneous world revolution, however, seems highly implausible. It is as a counter to this that Williams proposes militant particularism, which conceives of political struggle in one place giving rise to generalized struggle in other sites.

Another important aspect of prefigurative politics subject to criticism by Srnicek and Williams is its attempt to embody an emancipated, post-capitalist future in the here and now, that is, 'to enact the space of a non-capitalist world' (2016: 34). The problem, in their eyes, is that the drive to act out an emancipated future uses up activists' energy and so distracts them from the slow work of bringing about, in a painstaking and systematic way, a credible and permanent shift away from the capitalist order of things. While I have much sympathy within this criticism, Srnicek and Williams's own appeals to a post-capitalist world 'in which people are no longer bound to their jobs, but free to create their own lives' (Srnicek and Williams, 2016: 85–6), sounds overgeneralized and without concrete content. If, as they readily accept, 'neoliberalism constitutes our collective common sense, making us its subjects whether we believe in it or not' (p. 65), then any attempt to move beyond the neoliberal order will necessitate concrete concepts of a post-capitalist condition. While they stand opposed to specific attempts to instantiate the idea that 'another world is possible', Srnicek and Williams arguably run into the old Marxian problem of refusing to sketch out any details of a post-capitalist world order.

For Srnicek and Williams, contemporary work represents, in stark terms, a generalized condition of oppression. The project of the left, therefore, should not be to make work more tolerable, better remunerated or more fairly distributed. Instead, the core task is simply to abolish it. As we saw when considering Gorz's thought from the 1980s, neoliberalism has tended to make people look for meaning beyond the context of work. For Gorz, as for Srnicek and Williams, it is the enforced nature of paid work under capitalism that justifies is abolition: 'What does it mean to call for the end of work? By "work", we mean our jobs – or wage labour: the time and effort we sell to someone else in return for an income. This is a time that is not under our control, but under our bosses', managers' and employers' control' (Gorz, 2012: 85).

Mason (2015) labels his vision of post-capitalism 'project zero', which entails 'a zero-carbon energy system; the production of machines, products and services with zero marginal costs; and the reduction of necessary labour time as close as possible to zero' (p. 266). In similar terms, for Srnicek and Williams, 'the political project for the twenty-first century left must be to build an economy in which people are no longer dependent upon wage labour for survival' (2016: 105). Severing work and value – or accepting, as in Mason's argument, that this separation is already well underway – requires the introduction of a universal basic income (UBI) that would guarantee everyone sufficient means to lead a reasonably comfortable life irrespective of any work done. While this looks like a very attractive prospect, it is important to note that a techno-economic determinism underlies this argument: work *will* diminish, come what may. The current state of the debate appears to offer a stark choice between two varieties of progressive politics: one the one hand, an accelerationism that looks to transfer value distribution from work-based remuneration to a centralized UBI mechanism; and, on the other, a more traditional politics of the left, which remains rooted in the labour theory of value and champions the rights of the working class to reliable work, collective bargaining rights and workplace protections.

A fundamental problem with the former, accelerationist approach, as I see it, is that it proposes to defeat neoliberalism on its own ground. As I have discussed at length with regard to climate change (Elliott, 2016), the neoliberal order thrives by precipitating an ever-present sense of crisis. The currently prevalent discourse on automation and joblessness bears all the hallmarks of such crisis projection. Historically, earlier phases of technological innovation were invariably accompanied by similar concerns about mass unemployment, largely because it was difficult or impossible to predict how new employment would be created during of a wave of technologically driven job losses. Since the financial crisis starting in 2008, however, there is a growing consensus in leftist thinking that this time it is different and that 'societies are approaching an inflection point beyond which we foresee a rapid increase in the number of task domains in which machines have a competitive advantage over people earning wages' (Pierce *et al.*, 2019).

What the accelerationists fail to see, however, is the intrinsic incompatibility between the more or less total obsolescence of labour and the ability to make profits. The same fetishized futurism that characterizes Silicon Valley entrepreneurs is in evidence in the technological determinism of contemporary post-work leftists. At base, the optimism of the latter is predicated on the hope that the corporations that own the intellectual property rights to contemporary computer-based technologies will be pressured by the public or government into sharing the profits of their innovations in ways that do not involve labour. We only have to remind ourselves of the exponential rise in household debt, referenced earlier in this section, to see a more likely trajectory for the coming decades. The last three global economic crises (the dot com crisis of 2000–2, the financial crisis of 2007–9 and the coronavirus crisis of 2020) have all tended to exacerbate economic inequality and generalize precarity. Given this clear pattern, the idea that governments – especially in countries such as the UK and US where neoliberalism has long since become political common sense – will be won over by the idea of a UBI post-work platform is not credible.

What then is the alternative? My sense is that work cannot be left behind in any future progressive politics but rather reconceived along the lines of some elements in traditional socialism. It is essential that such reframing involve full recognition of what Harvey (2010) articulates as the fundamental contradiction in play in capitalism's drive for technological innovation:

> So here is the central contradiction: if social labour is the ultimate source of value and profit, then replacing it with machines or robotic labour makes no sense, either politically or economically. But we can see all too clearly what the mechanism is that heightens this contradiction to the point of crisis. Individual

> entrepreneurs or corporations see labour-saving innovation as critical to their profitability vis-à-vis competitors. This collectively undermines the possibility of profit. (Harvey, 2010: 104)

The intrinsic connection between socially necessary labour and capitalist profit, pointed out by Harvey here, is of itself a sufficient reason for rejecting the accelerationist platform. Another is the nature of capitalist production itself, insofar as it has precipitated a collapse in the earth's ecological systems. This is not the place to examine this second dimension in detail, something I did in a previous book (Elliott, 2016). It suffices to say that a programme of UBI, even if it were to be realized at a global scale, would do nothing in itself to chart a path towards ecological health and resilience. Once again, the key point to derive from the history of leftist politics is that the essential failing of capitalism does not lie within uneven distribution of value (as bad as that is) but rather consists in the very mode of value realized in capitalist production. It is not only people who are pointlessly used up under capitalism, but also the resources of 'nature' itself in a relentless search for profit which circumvents all barriers and transcends all viable thresholds.

For these two principal reasons, then, I believe the thesis of post-work accelerationism is a dead end for contemporary leftist theory and praxis. This brings us back to the central concern of this book: populism and the working class. Work matters to the working class not just because people have been hoodwinked into a puritanical work ethic. Work is a key way to demonstrate, in a social context, how we contribute to the common world inhabited by all. It is also a crucial way in which, as Sennett (2012) argues, we activate and hone our innate predisposition for cooperation. The need for social recognition – the drive to accrue social and cultural esteem – antedate capitalism and will remain in place after its demise.

Work is what we do to forge a common world at the most elementary, material level. Collaboration in the making of a common reality is, in political terms, the very ideal of democracy. Accordingly, any renewal of democracy that might arise out of the current wave of populism must, at the same time, involve a renewal rather than a definitive ending of the work world. Such a renewal must be the central concern of current leftist politics, and the way forward for progressive politics must remain in full, living consciousness of the generations of socialist struggle that have preceded it. It is only with this intergenerational consciousness, I contend, that the path to a viable and tenable future can be set out and embarked upon.

Conclusion

Populism and the culture of democracy

If a world beyond work is not viable, then the central task of the progressive left remains what it has always been: democratic control of material life including the conditions of work. Populism in the UK and US has been largely reviled by the progressive media as a sign that democratic civility has broken down or that liberal democracy itself is in terminal decline. Following this line of thought, the election of Trump and the Brexit referendum result represent a wholly undesirable recrudescence of mob rule. The basic problem with this analysis, as I have argued throughout this book, is that it mistakes symptoms for causes. As I have argued here, the underlying cause of contemporary populism in liberal democracies is neoliberal governance and the attendant disenfranchisement of the working class. It follows from this that populism has not suddenly arisen due to some caprice of the electorate but is rather the result of a generations-long restructuring of society that began in the 1970s. As a challenge to the purblind short-termism of most media analysis, therefore, my purpose in this book has been to offer a deeper, and hopefully more plausible, account of the roots of populism.

When Williams was writing *Culture and Society* (1958) the British working class had much more credible means at its disposal than it does today to express its dissatisfaction with the political and social status quo. Above all, Williams's key concern at this time was the very task identified at the end of the previous chapter, namely the renewal of democratic culture. Williams (1958) makes clear that, for him, democracy is not ultimately about a certain constitutional settlement, voting mechanism or set of political ideas. Instead it is a historically grounded collective demand of the working class. If this demand is seen to be denied, derided or deflected, the effects on political culture will become pervasively present: 'If people cannot have official democracy, they will have unofficial democracy, in any of its possible forms, from the armed revolt or riot, through the 'unofficial' strike or restriction of labour, to the quietest but most alarming form – a general sullenness and withdrawal of interest' (Williams, 1958: 315).

Forty years of neoliberal governance have left workers in liberal democracies arguably more vulnerable and disorganized than they have been for two hundred years. We may indeed, then, speak of a crisis of democracy, but this cannot be addressed effectively unless the roots of the crisis are accurately identified. The undermining of what might be called the culture of democracy has reached such a point that most workers believe they have little to no real power to influence, let alone control, their conditions of work. 'Sullenness and withdrawal of interest' is indeed a key feature of contemporary populism insofar as it involves a wholesale rejection of the established political class. I do not return to Williams here in order to hark back to some supposedly golden age of working-class political organization. Rather, I find Williams's work extremely useful as it articulates the core aspirations of democratic socialism with a clarity that is difficult to find in contemporary analysis. While, on the whole, populism has been taken to mean racially inflected mob rule in popular media, this interpretation can be readily contested. Thus, in the first chapter of this book, we considered Laclau's (2005) positive analysis of populism as embodying, in essence, the original democratic impulse to construct specific demands in the name of 'the people'.

Forty years of neoliberalism have also brought a thorough professionalization of liberal democratic politics, a process that has undoubtedly widened the gulf between political representatives and those they represent. One of Laclau's (2005) main points is that there is no settled agreement, no given identity relating to the represented, to 'the people': the demos is, and must remain, radically undetermined. To expand on this sense of class as indeterminate, we can also have recourse to E. P. Thompson's idea that collective class identity is not a fixed thing but rather something dynamic, something that happens to particular people in a particular situation. Viewed in this light, populism may be seen as a collective experience currently being lived through in liberal democracies, predominantly by the working class. Towards the end of his life Williams reiterated what he viewed as the fundamental intertwining of socialism and democracy:

> The link between socialism and popular democracy is literally the key to our future. Without it, the practice of socialism can degenerate to bureaucratic state forms or to the political and economic monopolies of command economies ... To move on to real sharing in all the decisions that affect our lives, not by some all-purpose mandate to others, but by direct participation and by accountable delegation, is the historic task of socialist democracy. (Williams, 1989: 285)

Three decades after Williams pointed out this need for shared decision-making as the key element of popular democracy, it would seem that we are further than ever from its realization. Many are convinced that the halcyon days of democracy lie behind rather than before us. The idea of 'illiberal democracy' first came to widespread attention (Zakaria, 1997) as a concept used to describe states where elections are held but there are conspicuous restrictions on civil liberties. Vladimir Putin's style of governance in Russia is paradigmatic of this trend, where elections are held but a one-party autocracy effectively holds sway. The recent political and electoral histories of Turkey and Hungary follow a similar pattern: a strongman demagogue who ushers in a series of constitutional reforms, usually by popular mandate, thereby consolidating power in the executive. While these developments are certainly of great significance, the notion of illiberal democracy is not particularly useful to us here, as the autocratic tendencies in a liberal democracy such as the UK are of a quite different kind. While there are genuine grounds for concern with respect to mass surveillance, the handling of domestic terrorism, and urban policing across liberal democracies, there is little to no family resemblance to the virulent ethnic nationalisms on display in Russia, Hungary or Turkey. The argument offered in this book, by contrast, is that the advent of neoliberal governance in the 1970s stalled the forward momentum towards a fully realized democratization of social existence. This reversing of democracy's 'long revolution' can be felt in all spheres.

The neoliberal repurposing of liberal democracy is generally offered to the people, perversely enough, as a breakthrough for individual liberty and freedom of choice. It usually involves privatization, whether of transportation systems, energy production or medical or educational provision. In the previous chapter we touched on another key domain: housing. One way to capture the shift is to note how the rights of the citizen have been transformed, on all fronts, into choices of the consumer. As Williams notes: 'It is an extraordinary word, "consumer". It is a way of seeing people as though they are either stomachs or furnaces' (1989: 216). In Marxian language, the conversion of the citizen into the consumer reflects the supremacy, in capitalism economics, of exchange value over use value. We see this logic at work in democratic electoral politics: voters are appealed to with respect to their individual economic interests: 'What are they offering me?' is the rhetorical question pressed upon the public. Politicians and the media dispute over which party has the more accurately costed manifesto, as though the only difference worth mentioning could be captured by a final figure on a balance sheet. The real problem with consumerist rhetoric, however, is that it induces collective passivity among the general public.

As often happens in outreach exercises of local government where the public is asked for input on a proposed urban renewal project, in general elections the electorate is given predetermined political programmes and asked to select A, B or C. The normalization of this process carries a pervasive and patently anti-democratic message: you don't get to propose solutions, so the best we can offer you is a set of predetermined policy positions to choose from. Once a choice has been made, however, parties and politicians are not readily held accountable to manifesto and campaign pledges. Promises made by pro-Brexit campaigners are an arch-example of this political unaccountability. All of this offers evidence of what Rancière calls a persistent 'hatred of democracy' or popular empowerment within the ecosystem of liberal democracy itself.

In Britain over the last two decades, this hatred of democracy has been most in evidence in the workings of New Labour. The problems that beset labour unions with regard to leadership hierarchy relative to rank-and-file membership are writ large in the case of a party historically dedicated to socialist transformation. Labour's success in the UK general elections of 1997, 2001 and 2005 was preceded and accompanied by reforms to the way the party functioned that could be broadly defined as anti-democratic in nature. Ideologically, New Labour's 'Third Way' marked the point at which neoliberalism became the received wisdom across British party politics, on the left as much as on the right. Leo Panitch and Colin Leys (2001) sum up this process in their detailed study of the rise of New Labour:

> The mass socialist and labour parties formed in Europe a century ago created institutional means through which working people could develop the capacity to govern their lives collectively, to learn to be active participants in democracy ... Little trace of it can any longer be found in social democratic parties in general, or New Labour in particular. New Labour still speaks in terms of developing capacities. But the capacities it explicitly seeks to develop are those of 'entrepreneurship' and 'competitiveness'. (Panitch and Leys, 2001: 290)

As explored in the first chapter of this book, according to Chantal Mouffe (2000) the formation of broad ideological consensus across the political spectrum has meant that political parties are no longer capable of capturing and channelling key differences of interest among the electorate. This has two key upshots: one the one hand, the kind of political indifference noted by Williams (1958); on the other, the formation and rapid success of new, anti-establishment parties. This happened in the UK with the rise – and post-referendum fall – of UKIP. UKIP is, in obvious ways, a populist party. Its leader for most of its existence, Nigel Farage, displays all the hallmark attributes of the demagogue: a desire to speak his mind, thereby purporting to represent what people really think, and scorning conventional political wisdom. When centrist democratic politics is so stage-managed and professionalized, the attractiveness to the public of such seemingly extempore self-presentation is not to be underestimated. In essence, however, a figure such as Farage offers no real means to 'get the country back' for those who feel disaffected from British party politics. Only a radical renewal of the culture of popular democracy can do that.

This renewal has to begin by overturning the political logic of neoliberalism. This requires a long, painstaking process of once again making credible and popular the socialist vision of spreading democratic control in all domains: work, housing, education, healthcare, child-rearing, energy production and transportation. As things stand, the majority of people in wealthy liberal democracies are plagued by their precarious economic position. Pervasive privatization of housing, healthcare and education are prime examples of how the political spirit level has been adjusted under neoliberal governance so that individuals take primary responsibility for their own well-being. Anything else is derided as shirking and freeloading. Forty years of public policy directed by this ideology has precipitated social crisis on many fronts: unsustainable levels of personal debt, insecurity of employment, persistent inequalities in educational outcomes and unaffordable housing costs. None of these issues can be fixed within the neoliberal ambit because of an ingrained attachment to austerity economics when it comes to public services.

While New Labour certainly did fund public services – particularly health and education – relatively generously over three successive terms of office, it also ideologically weakened the sense of collective social responsibility by promoting an ethos of individualized entrepreneurship. It also paved the way towards populism by abandoning its identification with the interests of the working class. It was under Blair that the Labour Party was truly severed from its roots in the trade union movement. According to Panitch and Leys: '[By 1997] Labour's days as the political wing of a broad-based social movement, seeking to educate public opinion and to lead a popular drive for social transformation, were clearly over' (2001: 236). It was only with the 2019 UK general election that the full extent of British working-class disenchantment with the Labour Party became evident, as the party's 'red wall' constituencies in northern England fell to the Conservatives in record numbers (see Baston, 2019). This confluence of the electoral failure of the UK's traditional leftist party and widespread support for the kind of populist sentiment expressed by working-class Brexit voters makes clear both the dire need and the scale of the challenge in working to renew democratic political culture.

Brexit and the return of 'mob rule'

Having cofounded modern cultural studies in the late 1950s and become one of the most influential figures of the British New Left in the 1960s, Raymond Williams spent the last decade of his life (he died in 1988) trying to make sense of the neoliberal counter-revolution ushered in by successive Conservative governments. For leftist thinkers of Williams's generation there was a pervasive disbelief that this could even be happening. In the late 1950s and early 1960s, when the likes of Hoggart (1957), Williams (1958) and E. P. Thompson (1968) published their seminal studies of British working-class culture, it seemed clear which way the tide of history was flowing. It was apparent to them all that there was something extraordinary, historically unparalleled, in the development of British working-class political and social organization since the 1820s.

But there was also a vivid sense that the nature of this organization was shifting, perhaps breaking up, particularly under pressures exerted by changes in popular media, communications and entertainment. When Margaret Thatcher first came to power in 1979, therefore, the coherence of British working-class culture had already been much diminished. Since the 1973 oil crisis and the global economic recession that ensued, domestic politics in Britain had been chaotic. This chaos culminated in the notorious 'winter of discontent' of 1978/79, when tens of thousands of public sector workers staged strikes in opposition to the Labour government's attempts to restrain wage increases.

The popular press successfully portrayed union actions as irresponsible and effectively holding the country to ransom in their efforts to increase wages. Following a vote of confidence in early 1979, the Labour minority government was obliged to call a general election which was lost to the Tories. The stage was thus set for the Thatcher government and its anti-union rhetoric of hard choices and general austerity. The eighteen years of Conservative rule in Britain that was to follow set about rooting out most of the elements of social democracy that had been achieved since 1945. Following the hard-line government response to the miners' strike of 1984/85, Thatcher's 'no alternative' mantra was thoroughly internalized and this led to the mass demoralization of organized labour in the UK. Writing in the shadow of these developments, Williams diagnosed a general retreat from the public into the private sphere:

> It's something like this: that the identity that is really offered to us is a new kind of freedom in that area of our lives that we have staked out inside these wider determinations and constraints. It is private. It involves, in its immedi-

> ate definition, a good deal of evident consumption. Much of it is centred on the home itself, the dwelling-place. Much of it, in those terms, enlists many of the most productive, imaginative impulses and activities of people – moreover sanely so, as against the competing demands of orthodox politics. Because what you put in, in effort, in this way, you usually get to live with and have its value. (Williams, 1989: 171)

It's hard to miss the rather elegiac tone to Williams's comments here. But there is also indignation and defiance. And hope. Through all his writing a certain faith in the power of working people to forge effective and vital solidarities is apparent. Even as the public turns inwards to the comparative safety of the domestic environment, Williams is able to see this as a basically sound and healthy impulse. But the privatization of common life is, without doubt, ultimately dispiriting for him. Above all, it marks the defeat of social democracy, understood as the effective sharing of decisions and actions to create a common material existence.

This is the condition that has prevailed in liberal democracies such as the UK since the early 1980s. It has allowed the party system and the political class as a whole gradually to replace the popular will with the corporate will. Just as leading corporations have turned to neoliberal government to tame the collective power of organized labour, so have political parties increasingly sought to win backing for their policies from the business sector. This was nowhere more apparent than in the Brexit negotiations, where big business impatiently pressed government for certainty and predictability for future economic transactions – as though the purpose of politics was chiefly or exclusively a matter of facilitating international trade. Little wonder that, in this political climate, the British working class seized on the EU referendum as a unique chance to puncture this self-satisfied political-corporate enterprise.

Since the idea of populism hit the headlines following the Brexit vote and the election of Trump, the notion that it is driven by a marginalized or ignored working-class constituency has gained traction. While this assertion has some truth to it, it is insufficient without a richer, historically deeper and more nuanced account of how this constituency came to be what it is. William Davies (2016) raises a crucial question about the agency driving contemporary populism: what does it hope to achieve? As is generally the case when speaking of social class, so too it is important not to assume that some homogeneous set of reasons motivates contemporary populism. Davies questions whether those traditionally Labour voters in Britain who voted in favour of Brexit actually meant to achieve anything at all:

> Amongst people who have utterly given up on the future, political movements don't need to promise any desirable and realistic change. If anything, they are

> more comforting and trustworthy if predicated on the notion that the future is beyond rescue, for that chimes more closely with people's private experiences ... Brexit was never really articulated as a viable policy, and only ever as a destructive urge, which some no doubt now feel guilty for giving way to. (Davies, 2016: 22)

While this buyer's remorse hypothesis may seem credible, it ultimately rings hollow. Indifference to the political future is most likely to produce apathy and indifference, whereas the EU referendum and the 2016 US presidential campaign created genuine excitement and widespread engagement. Davies's argument really belongs to that genre of writing about the working class as an unenlightened mob, which was identified by Williams (1958) to be present in political thought throughout the history of modern democracy. The fact that Davies writes as a leftist doesn't make any difference on this score. It is all too easy for intellectuals of the left to say 'yes, we recognize why people are angry under neoliberalism; but they have no idea how they can really work towards a better political order'.

The question, then, is whether contemporary populism gives voice to the despair or hope of the liberal democratic electorate. Williams expressed his own underlying faith in popular democracy as a matter of 'an ingrained and indestructible yet also changing embodiment of the possibilities of common life' (1989: 322). His socialism is a question of hope in the ultimate irreversibility of the 'long revolution'. The commonality of human life touches on the very foundations of political order. Aristotle (2009) famously claimed that the city-state or polis existed for the sake of the collective good life rather than mere economic expediency. This teleological explanation of political order ties it to a collective pursuit of the good. Populism, in this light, can be seen in terms of a fundamental demand that the good of all be the active concern of all within the political community.

The path of populism

How, then, should we view the future of populism? Does it point in specific directions or does it merely represent some kind of hiatus in the normal path of democratic political development? The underlying purpose of the analysis offered in this book has been to arrive at a historically and materially adequate theory of contemporary populism, with particular emphasis on the condition of British politics following the Brexit referendum result. Between 2016 and 2017 the UK underwent a protracted period of political crisis and virtual paralysis under Theresa May as prime minister. Throughout this period, public debate remained stuck in the binary terms of the EU referendum: an anti-establishment 'just get it done' Brexit bloc on the one side; and an anti-Brexit constituency that largely defended its position on the basis of anticipated adverse economic consequences.

Such a situation constitutes a case of what the French thinker Jean-François Lyotard (1988) called a 'differend': a dispute lacking common terms of exchange. Pro-Brexit discourse clearly displays elements of a nostalgic yearning for a pre-globalized sense of Britain (just as Trump's vision of America harks back to an image of the country as radically autarchic). This involves constructing the nation state as an imagined community of untrammelled self-determination that is – given the actual conditions of transnational neoliberal capitalism – a historical impossibility. The anti-Brexit discourse, on the other hand, appeals to a laissez-faire common sense of openness and enlightened capitalist prosperity. It recognizes, to a degree at least, the sharpening inequality present in contemporary liberal democracies but possesses a fundamental faith in the 'no alternative' logic of neoliberalism.

Now that the UK has formally left the European Union, breaking through the binary opposition of nationalist autarky versus corporate-led neoliberal internationalism requires constructing quite a different political imaginary. My argument throughout this book has been that such a political space should be looked for by picking up the largely severed threads of a socialist heritage. This is necessary as there is no way, in my view, to bridge the gap between the alternatives of reactionary nationalism and laissez-faire internationalism currently on offer. According to Lyotard, the whole point about a 'differend' is that no common language can be found in which a compromise between opponents can be struck. Recalling Mouffe's (2000) argument, this is why democracies require a plurality of parties that can respectively articulate the necessary 'agonistics' of political dispute. There is a basic point about the nature of modern liberal democracy at stake here. The plurality of parties is not simply a matter of ideological degrees of difference. The workers' movement, which was the historical engine of democracy, did not advance its demands largely as an appeal to the better instincts of the economically and ideologically dominant class. Instead, these demands were advanced antagonistically, through the demonstrated power of collective action.

In this light, contemporary populism should not be seen as a sign that democracy is degenerating, even though it does point to a certain crisis in the original sense of a moment of decision. Put otherwise, it indicates that the originating spirit of democracy is attempting to find new expression and thereby to reassert itself. Saying this in no way entails accepting at face value the nationalistic or even neo-imperialistic sentiments of some in the pro-Brexit wing of the British Conservative Party, still less the vitriolic verbiage of a Donald Trump or any other contemporary demagogue. Reactionary populism can be readily accepted as a nascent form of fascism, while still recognizing that the populist sentiment, more generally, is the original source of democratic political community.

As I hope to have demonstrated in this book, a fundamental ambivalence about the political legitimacy of 'the people' has characterized modern democratic politics from its inception. The world in which I grew up, in 1970s northern England, marked a point in social and political history in which the 'levelling' impact of working-class culture had reached something of a zenith. Levels of income equality reflected this, as did, to some degree, educational and vocational opportunity. Certainly, at the same time deep prejudices based on race, gender and sexual orientation remained very much in place. In my lifetime, however, the condition of the working class has drastically worsened. While most attention is given in this regard to heightened economic inequality, my argument throughout this book has focused, rather, on the psychological, social and cultural devaluation of working-class life. It is the consequent resentment generated by this devaluation, I hold, that is the root cause of contemporary populism.

We can connect this to one of the common tropes of the contemporary analysis of populism: hatred of 'the establishment'. As Richard Hoggart documented in 1957, the British working class was indelibly characterized by a scornful suspicion of their 'betters', feeling that the game of social advancement was rigged by those in charge, who were only in it for themselves (2009). Attempting to play by the established rules would entail you becoming 'one of them', that is, betraying your class in an attempt to get above yourself. But it was just this strong adhesive of working-class solidarity and loyalty to 'one's own' that was deliberately dissolved by the relentlessly individualistic entrepreneurialism of neoliberal governance from the early 1980s on. It is this process, I think, which has run its course with the emergence of contemporary populism. What more effective way of demonstrating this than seeing the limits of neoliberal governance in the face of the communitarianism required to respond to a global pandemic?

If populism stems from resentment at the disempowerment of the people under neoliberal democracy, then the only viable response is to begin the slow and painstaking process of rebuilding grassroots democracy. This takes many forms: bringing certain vital sectors and utilities back into some form of collective ownership; renewing and expanding the role of trades unions and other organized forms of worker self-representation; reforming social, educational and health services so that all people can enjoy as much freedom from material burden as possible; limiting the power of the finance sector so that it does not continue to undermine the productive economy and its benefits to the majority. Above all, the dignity of people seen and respected as capable of self-governance must be restored. The alternative, all too evident in the reactionary leaders in putative liberal democracies today, is a potential slide into reactionary authoritarianism that uses fear of other countries to instil panic and insularity within the nation state.

Populism, then, ultimately calls for a renewal of the spirit of democracy through every organ of the body politic. This body has been enervated by four decades of neoliberalism. To grow again, dignity and respect must be regained by the people, so that democracy stands for more than a spectre of human rights predicated on inexorably improving gross domestic product. For this to happen, the political class must change its own nature, becoming thereby much more plausibly representative of the people. It must not simply profess to listen but be prepared to have civil society set the terms of debate. Above all, the working class must be renewed by a restructuring of the economy in line with worthwhile employment that allows workers pride in their work and a credible ability to develop as a person over a lifetime. Pandemic conditions have given rise to an unwonted level of political respect for 'essential workers', most obviously those working in the health sector. Let us hope this is a sign that, in future, we can reform our political, economic and ecological systems in line with what is truly necessary to a worthwhile and dignified life of the whole of society.

References

Adams, R. 2019. Vice-Chancellors Paid £500,000 or More at Six Universities in England. *Guardian*, 12 February. Available at: www.theguardian.com/education/2019/feb/12/vice-chancellors-pay-universities-england-2017-18 (accessed 12 October 2020).

Adorno, T. 1994. *The Stars Down to Earth and Other Essays on the Irrational in Society*. New York: Routledge.

Adorno, T. 2001 [1976]. *The Culture Industry: Selected Essays on Mass Culture*. London: Routledge.

Arendt, H. 2018 [1958]. *The Human Condition*, 2nd edn. Chicago, IL: University of Chicago Press.

Aristotle. 2009. *Politics*. Oxford: Oxford University Press.

Arnold, M. 2010. *Culture and Anarchy and Other Writings*. Cambridge: Cambridge University Press.

Baston, L. 2019. This Defeat Leaves Labour Support Unrecognisable from 35 Years Ago. *Guardian*, 13 December. Available at: www.theguardian.com/commentisfree/2019/dec/13/defeat-labour-support-unrecognisable-30-years-michael-foot (accessed 12 October 2020).

Bell, D. 1956. *Work and Its Discontents*. Boston, MA: Beacon Press.

Benhabib, S. 1996. 'Toward a Deliberative Model of Democratic Legitimacy'. In: S. Benhabib (ed.), *Democracy and Difference: Contesting the Boundaries of the Political*. Princeton, NJ: Princeton University Press, pp. 67–94.

Blair, T. 1999. Labour Party Conference: Tony Blair's Full Speech. *Guardian*, 28 September. Available at: www.theguardian.com/politics/1999/sep/28/labourconference.labour14 (accessed 6 October 2020).

Brenner, N. 2011. *Cities for People, Not for Profit: Critical Urban Theory and the Right to the City*. New York: Routledge.

Bush, G. W. 2001. President Bush Addresses the Nation. *Washington Post*, 20 September. Available at: www.washingtonpost.com/wp-srv/nation/specials/attacked/transcripts/bushaddress_092001.html (accessed 6 October 2020).

Bush, G. W. 2002. Text of President Bush's 2002 State of the Union Address. *Washington Post*, 29 January. Available at: www.washingtonpost.com/wp-srv/onpolitics/transcripts/sou012902.htm (accessed 6 October 2020).

Carlyle, T. 2010. *Latter-Day Pamphlets*. Cambridge: Cambridge University Press.

Cederström, C. and A. Spicer. 2015. *The Wellness Syndrome*. London: Verso.

Chiripanhura, B. and N. Wolf. 2019. *Long-term Trends in UK Employment: 1861 to 2018*. Available at: www.ons.gov.uk/economy/nationalaccounts/uksectorac

counts/compendium/economicreview/april2019/longtermtrendsinukemploymen t1861to2018#the-evolution-of-sectoral-distribution-of-employment (accessed 8 October 2020).

Collini, S. 2018. *Speaking of Universities*. London: Verso.

Dardot, P. and C. Laval. 2014. *The New Way of the World: On Neoliberal Society*. London: Verso.

Davies, W. 2015. *The Happiness Industry: How the Government and Big Business Sold Us Well-Being*. London: Verso.

Davies, W. 2016. 'Thoughts on the Sociology of Brexit'. In: Verso (ed.), *The Brexit Crisis: A Verso Report*. London: Verso, pp. 15–26.

Dunn, M. and J. Walker 2016. *Union Membership in the United States*. Available at: www.bls.gov/spotlight/2016/union-membership-in-the-united-states/pdf/union-membership-in-the-united-states.pdf (accessed 8 October 2020).

Eatwell, R. and M. Goodwin. 2018. *National Populism: The Revolt Against Liberal Democracy*. London: Pelican.

Elliott, B. 2010. *Constructing Community: Configurations of the Social in Contemporary Philosophy and Urbanism*. Lanham, MD: Rowman & Littlefield.

Elliott, B. 2016. *Natural Catastrophe: Climate Change and Neoliberal Governance*. Edinburgh: Edinburgh University Press.

Engels, F. 2003. *Socialism: Utopian and Scientific*. Available at: www.marxists.org/archive/marx/works/1880/soc-utop/index.htm (accessed 12 October 2020).

Foucault, M. 1995 [1975]. *Discipline and Punish: The Birth of the Prison*. New York: Vintage.

Foucault, M. 2008. *The Birth of Biopolitics: Lectures at the Collège de France 1978–1979*. New York: Picador.

Friedman, M. 2002 [1962]. *Capitalism and Freedom: Fortieth Anniversary Edition*. Chicago, IL: Chicago University Press.

Friedman, M. and R. Friedman. 1990. *Free to Choose: A Personal Statement*. New York: Houghton Mifflin Harcourt.

Fromm, E. 2001 [1942]. *The Fear of Freedom*. New York: Routledge.

Giddens, A. 1998. *The Third Way: The Renewal of Social Democracy*. Cambridge: Polity.

Gorz, A. 2012. *Capitalism, Socialism, Ecology*. London: Verso.

Graeber, D. 2013. On the Phenomenon of Bullshit Jobs: A Work Rant. *Strike! Magazine*, issue 3, August. Available at: www.strike.coop/bullshit-jobs/ (accessed 12 October 2020).

Graham, S. 2010. *Cities Under Siege: The New Military Urbanism*. London: Verso.

Guardian. 2016. EU Referendum: Full Results and Analysis. *Guardian*, 23 June. Available at: www.theguardian.com/politics/ng-interactive/2016/jun/23/eu-refer endum-live-results-and-analysis (accessed 11 October 2020).

Gumbrell-McCormick, R. 2011. European Trade Unions and 'Atypical' Workers. *Industrial Relations Journal*, 42(3), 293–310.

Gutmann, A. and D. Thompson. 1996. *Democracy and Disagreement*. Cambridge, MA: Harvard University Press.

Habermas, J. 1985. *The Theory of Communicative Action*. Vol. 1: *Reason and Rationalization of Society*. Boston, MA: Beacon Press.

Habermas, J. 1990. *Moral Consciousness and Communicative Action*. Cambridge: Polity Press.

Handler, J. F. 2003. Social Citizenship and Workfare in the US and Western Europe: From Status to Contract. *Journal of European Social Policy*, 13(3), 229–43.

Harris, J. 2019. Working-class Voters Desert Labour as 'Red Wall' Crumbles. *Guardian*, 13 December. Available at: www.theguardian.com/politics/2019/dec/13/working-class-voters-desert-labour-stoke-on-trent-england-red-wall (accessed 6 October 2020).

Harris, J. and J. Domokos. 2019. We Spent 10 Years Talking to People. Here's What It Taught Us About Britain. *Guardian*, 3 December. Available at: www.theguardian.com/news/2019/dec/03/anywhere-but-westminster-vox-pops-understanding-uk-political-landscape (accessed 6 October 2020).

Harvey, D. 2005. *A Brief History of Neoliberalism*. Oxford: Oxford University Press.

Harvey, D. 2010. *The Enigma of Capital: And the Crises of Capitalism*. Oxford: Oxford University Press.

Harvey, D. 2012. *Rebel Cities: From the Right to the City to the Urban Revolution*. London: Verso.

Harvey, D. 2014. *Seventeen Contradictions and the End of Capitalism*. London: Profile Books.

Hayek, F. 2007 [1944]. *The Road to Serfdom*. Chicago, IL: Chicago University Press.

Hayek, F. 2011 [1960]. *The Constitution of Liberty*. Chicago, IL: Chicago University Press.

Heying, C. 2010. *Brew to Bikes: Portland's Artisan Economy*. Portland, OR: Ooligan Press.

Hill, H. 1996. The Problem of Race in American Labor History. *Reviews in American History*, 24(2), 189–208.

Hoggart, R. 2009 [1957]. *The Uses of Literacy: Aspects of Working-Class Life*. London: Penguin.

Horkheimer M. and T. Adorno. 1997 [1944]. *The Dialectics of Enlightenment*. London: Verso.

HSE. 2019. *Work-related Stress, Anxiety or Depression Statistics in Great Britain, 2019*. Available at: www.hse.gov.uk/statistics/causdis/stress.pdf (accessed 12 October 2020).

Inman, P. 2020. UK Jobless Rate 'Could Near 15% in Second Coronavirus Wave'. *Guardian*, 7 July. Available at: www.theguardian.com/business/2020/jul/07/uk-jobless-rate-coronavirus-oecd-unemployment (accessed12 October 2020).

Jacobs, J. 1989 [1961]. *The Death and Life of the Great American City*. London: Vintage.

Jin, J. and S. J. Ball. 2019. Precarious Success and the Conspiracy of Reflexivity: Questioning the 'Habitus Transformation' of Working-Class Students at Elite Universities. *Critical Studies in Education*, 1–16.

Jones, O. 2016. *Chavs: The Demonization of the Working Class*. London: Verso.

Judis, J. B. 2016. *The Populist Explosion: How the Great Recession Transformed American and European Politics*. New York: Columbia Global Reports.

Kaminer, W. 2011. The Hypocrisy of Occupy Wall Street. *The Atlantic*, 18 November. Available at: www.theatlantic.com/national/archive/2011/11/the-hypocrisy-of-occupy-wall-street/248675/ (accessed12 October 2020).

Klein, N. 2007. *The Shock Doctrine*. London: Allen Lane.

Lacan, J. 2006 [1966]. *Écrits: The First Complete Edition in English*. New York: Norton.

Laclau, E. 2005. *On Populist Reason*. London: Verso.

Laclau, E. and C. Mouffe. 1985. *Hegemony and Socialist Strategy*. London: Verso.

Laclau, E. and C. Mouffe. 2005. *Hegemony and Socialist Strategy: Towards a Radical Democratic Politics*. London: Verso.

Lawrence, E. 2016. *Gender and Trade Unions*. London: Routledge.

Le Bon, G. 2009 [1895]. *Psychology of Crowds*. Southampton: Sparkling Books.

Lefebvre, H. 2002 [1961]. *Critique of Everyday Life: Volume II*. London: Verso.

Lyotard, J.-F. 1988. *The Differend: Phrases in Dispute*. Minneapolis, MN: University of Minnesota Press.

Marotta, S. and C. Heying. 2018. 'Interrogating Localism: What does "Made in Portland" really Mean?' In: S. Luckman and N. Thomas (eds), *Craft Economies*. London: Bloomsbury pp. 141–9.

Marx, K. 2010. 'Value, Price, and Profit'. In: J. Sitton (ed.), *Marx Today: Selected Works and Recent Debates*. New York: Palgrave Macmillan, pp. 95–122.

Marx, K. and F. Engels. 2004 [1848]. *The Communist Manifesto*. London: Penguin.

Mason, P. 2014. Thomas Piketty's *Capital*: Everything You Need to Know About the Surprise Bestseller. *Guardian*, 28 April. www.theguardian.com/books/2014/apr/28/thomas-piketty-capital-surprise-bestseller (accessed 7 October 2020).

Mason, P. 2015. *PostCapitalism: A Guide to Our Future*. London: Allen Lane.

McChesney, R. 2015. *Rich Media, Poor Democracy: Communication Politics in Dubious Times*. New York: New Press.

McNay, L. 2009. Self as Enterprise: Dilemmas of Control and Resistance in Foucault's *The Birth of Biopolitics*. *Theory, Culture, and Society*, 26(6), 55–77.

McRobbie, A. 2016. *Be Creative: Making a Living in the New Culture Industries*. Cambridge: Polity.

Merrick, R. 2017. Ukip: A Timeline of the Party's Turbulent History. *Independent*, 29 September. Available at: www.independent.co.uk/news/uk/politics/ukip-timeline-party-westminster-alan-sked-nigel-farage-conference-key-events-brexit-leadership-a7974606.html (accessed 12 October 2020).

Merrifield, A. 2014. *The New Urban Question*. London: Pluto Press.

Mill, J. S. 1989 [1859]. *On Liberty and Other Writings*. Cambridge: Cambridge University Press.

Mill, J. S. 2008 [1848]. *Principles of Political Economy; and Chapters on Socialism*. London: Penguin.

Miller-Idriss, C. and H. Pilkington, eds. 2019. *Gender and the Radical and Extreme Right*. New York: Routledge.

Mingay, G. E. 1997. *Parliamentary Enclosure in England: An Introduction to Its Causes, Incidence and Impact 1750–1850*. New York: Longman.

Mitchell, D. 2003. *The Right to the City: Social Justice and the Fight for Public Space*. New York: Guilford Press.

Morris, C. 2019. Brexit: What Does the Deal Say About Workers' Rights? BBC News, 19 October. Available at: www.bbc.com/news/uk-politics-50096400 (accessed 12 October 2020).

Mouffe, C. 2000. *The Democratic Paradox*. London: Verso.

Mouffe, C. 2005. *On the Political*. New York: Routledge.

Mudde, C. 2004. The Populist Zeitgeist. *Government and Opposition*, 39(3), 541–63.

Mudde, C. 2018. How Populism Became the Concept That Defines Our Age. *Guardian*, 22 November. Available at www.theguardian.com/commentisfree/2018/nov/22/populism-concept-defines-our-age (accessed 29 October 2020).

Mudde, C. and C. R. Kaltwasser, eds. 2012. *Populism in Europe and the Americas: Threat or Corrective for Democracy?* Cambridge: Cambridge University Press.

Murie, A. 2016. *The Right to Buy?: Selling off Public and Social Housing*. Bristol: Policy Press.

Mutikani, L. 2020. Coronavirus Deals U.S. Economy Great Depression-Like Job Losses, High Unemployment. Reuters, 8 May. Available at: www.reuters.com/article/us-usa-economy/coronavirus-deals-u-s-economy-great-depression-like-job-losses-high-unemployment-idUSKBN22K1NS (accessed 12 October 2020).

Norris, P. 2016. It's Not Just Trump. Authoritarian Populism Is Rising across the West. Here's Why. *Washington Post*, 11 March. Available at www.washingtonpost.com/news/monkey-cage/wp/2016/03/11/its-not-just-trump-authoritarian-populism-is-rising-across-the-west-heres-why/ (accessed 29 October 2020).

Norris, P. and R. Ingelhart. 2019. *Cultural Backlash: Trump, Brexit, and Authoritarian Populism*. Cambridge: Cambridge University Press.

Nozick, R. 2013 [1974]. *Anarchy, State, and Utopia*. New York: Basic Books.

Office for National Statistics. 2019. *Household Debt in Great Britain: April 2016 to March 2018*. Available at: www.ons.gov.uk/peoplepopulationandcommunity/personalandhouseholdfinances/incomeandwealth/bulletins/householddebtingreatbritain/april2016tomarch2018 (accessed 12 October 2020).

Panitch, L. and C. Leys. 2001. *The End of Parliamentary Socialism: From New Left to New Labour*. London: Verso.

Pierce, J., M. Lawhon and T. McCreary. 2019. From Precarious Work to Obsolete Labour? Implications of Technological Disemployment for Geographical Scholarship. *Geografiska Annaler: Series B, Human Geography*, 101(2), 84–101.

Piketty, T. 2013. *Le capital au XXI siècle* [*Capital in the Twenty-First Century*]. Paris: Éditions du Seuil.

Pitts, F. H., L. Lombardozzi and N. Warner. 2017. The Future of Social Democracy: Speenhamland, Automation and the Basic Income: A Warning from History? *Renewal. A Journal of Social Democracy*, 25(3–4), 145–55.

Rancière, J. 1991 [1987]. *The Ignorant Schoolmaster: Five Lessons in Intellectual Emancipation*. Stanford, CA: Stanford University Press.

Rancière, J. 1999 [1995]. *Disagreement*. Minneapolis, MN: Minnesota University Press.

Rancière, J. 2004 [1983]. *The Philosopher and His Poor*. Durham, NC: Duke University Press.

Rancière, J. 2006. *Hatred of Democracy*. London: Verso.

Rancière, J. 2012. *Proletarian Nights: The Workers' Dream in Nineteenth-Century France*. London: Verso.

Rancière, J. 2016. 'The Populism that is Not to be Found'. In: A. Badiou, J. Butler, G. Didi-Huberman, S. Khiari, J. Rancière and P. Bourdieu, *What is a People?* New York: Columbia University Press, 2016, pp. 101–6.

Ravitch, D. 2014. *Reign of Error: The Hoax of the Privatization Movement and the Danger to America's Public Schools*. New York: Vintage.

Ravitch, D. 2016. *The Death and Life of the Great American School System: How Testing and Choice Are Undermining Education*. New York: Basic Books.

Rawls, J. 1999. *A Theory of Justice*. Cambridge, MA: Harvard University Press.

Rawstorne, T. 2011. Rabble Without a Cause. *Mail on Sunday*, 29 October. Available at: www.dailymail.co.uk/news/article-2054912/Occupy-London-St-Pauls-protest-rabble-cause.html (accessed 12 October 2020).

Reuters, 2019. U.S. Household Debt in Four Charts. Reuters, 13 November. Available at: https://uk.reuters.com/article/us-usa-fed-debt-charts-graphic/us-household-debt-in-four-charts-idUKKBN1XN2OH (accessed 12 October 2020).

Rothman, L. 2016. Why Bill Clinton Signed the Welfare Reform Bill, as Explained in 1996. *Time*, 19 August. Available at: https://time.com/4446348/welfare-reform-20-years/ (accessed 12 October 2020).

Sartre, J.-P. 1995 [1948]. *Anti-Semite and Jew: An Exploration of the Etiology of Hate*. New York: Schocken Books.

Schmitt, C. 2005 [1922]. *Political Theology: Four Chapters on the Concept of Sovereignty*. Chicago, IL: Chicago University Press.

Sennett, R. 2006. *The Culture of the New Capitalism*. New Haven, CT: Yale University Press.

Sennett, R. 2008. *The Craftsman*. London: Penguin.

Sennett, R. 2012. *Together: The Rituals, Pleasures and Politics of Cooperation*. New Haven, CT: Yale University Press.

Sennett, R. 2017 [1977]. *The Fall of Public Man*. Fortieth Anniversary edn. London: Norton & Norton.

Sennett, R. and J. Cobb. 1972. *The Hidden Injuries of Class*. New York: Knopf.

Siméon, O. 2017. *Robert Owen's Experiment at New Lanark: From Paternalism to Socialism*. London: Palgrave Macmillan.

Simmel, G. 1971 [1903]. *On Individuality and Social Forms*. Chicago, IL: Chicago University Press.

Smith, N. 1996. *The New Urban Frontier: Gentrification and the Revanchist City*. London: Routledge.

Sparrow, A. and B. Neild. 2013. Local Elections 2013: Friday 3 May as It Happened. *Guardian*, 3 May. www.theguardian.com/politics/blog/2013/may/03/local-elections-2013-live-blog (accessed 6 October 2020).

Srnicek, N. and A. Williams. 2016. *Inventing the Future: Postcapitalism and a World Without Work*. London: Verso.

Syal, R. and H. Stewart. 2018. Workers get new rights in overhaul but zero-hours contracts remain. *Guardian*, 17 December. Available at: www.theguardian.com/law/2018/dec/17/workers-get-new-rights-in-overhaul-but-zero-hours-contracts-remain (accessed 12 October 2020).

The Equality Trust. 2017. How Has Inequality Changed? Available at: www.equalitytrust.org.uk/how-has-inequality-changed (accessed 8 October 2020).

Thompson, D. 1984. *The Chartists*. London: Temple Smith.

Thompson, D. 2015. *The Dignity of Chartism*. London: Verso.

Thompson, E. P. 1968 [1963]. *The Making of the English Working Class*. London: Pelican.

Tomlinson, D. 2017. Trade Union Membership Has Fallen Further Than Ever Before. Resolution Foundation, 31 May. Available at: www.resolutionfoundation.org/comment/trade-union-membership-has-fallen-further-than-ever-before/ (accessed 8 October 2020).

Traverso, E. 2019. *The New Faces of Fascism: Populism and the Far Right*. London: Verso.

UK Department for Business, Energy and Industrial Strategy. 2018. *Trade Union Membership: Statistical Bulletin*. Available at: https://assets.publishing.service.gov.uk/government/uploads/system/uploads/attachment_data/file/805268/trade-union-membership-2018-statistical-bulletin.pdf (accessed 9 October 2020).

UK Parliament. 2013. *Parliament and Europe: The EEC and the Single European Act*. Available at: www.parliament.uk/about/living-heritage/evolutionofparliament/legislativescrutiny/parliament-and-europe/overview/britain-and-eec-to-single-european-act/ (accessed 8 October 2020).

UK Parliament. 2020. Student Loan Statistics. Available at https://commonslibrary.parliament.uk/research-briefings/sn01079/ (accessed 29 October 2020).

UK Parliament. n.d. *Enclosing the Land*. Available at: www.parliament.uk/about/living-heritage/transformingsociety/towncountry/landscape/overview/enclosingland/ (accessed 7 October 2020).

Veblen, T. 2009 [1899]. *The Theory of the Leisure Class*. Oxford: Oxford University Press.

Wheatley, D. 2017. Autonomy in Paid Work and Employee Subjective Well-being. *Work and Occupations*, 44(3), 296–328.

Williams, R. 1958. *Culture and Society: 1780–1950*. London: Chatto & Windus.

Williams, R. 1961. *The Long Revolution*. London: Chatto & Windus.

Williams, R. 1973. *The Country and the City*. Oxford: Oxford University Press.

Williams, R. 1983. *Writing in Society*. London: Verso.

Williams, R. 1989. *Resources of Hope: Culture, Democracy, Socialism*. London: Verso.

Williams, R. 2005. *Culture and Materialism*. London: Verso.

Wood, E. M. 2016. *Democracy Against Capitalism: Renewing Historical Materialism*. London: Verso.

Wood, L. J. 2014. *Direct Action, Deliberation, and Diffusion: Collective Action after the WTO Protests in Seattle* (Cambridge Studies in Contentious Politics). Cambridge: Cambridge University Press.

Young, I. M. 2010. *Inclusion and Democracy*. Oxford: Oxford University Press.

Young, I. M. 2011. *Justice and the Politics of Difference*. Princeton, NJ: Princeton University Press.

Zakaria, F. 1997. The Rise of Illiberal Democracy. *Foreign Affairs*, 76(6), 22–43.

Index